GW00758598

MY GUY

The Photostories

The Photostories

Frank Hopkinson

PORTICO

First published in the United Kingdom in 2007 by
Portico
10 Southcombe Street,
London W14 0RA

An imprint of Anova Books Company Ltd.

Copyright © *My Guy* magazine/Frank Hopkinson, 2007
My Guy magazine is a trademark of Perfectly Formed Publishing,
Bas du Chemin, La Motte es Ribourdouille, Plessala, 22330, France

The moral right of the author has been asserted.

All rights reserved. No part of this publication may be reproduced, stored in a retrieval system,
or transmitted in any form or by any means electronic, mechanical, photocopying, recording or
otherwise, without the prior written permission of the copyright owner.

The photostories in this book were originally published between 1978 and 1999.

ISBN 10: 1 90060 3217 3
ISBN 13: 9781906032173

A CIP catalogue record for this book is available from the British Library.

10 9 8 7 6 5 4 3 2 1

Printed in Italy

MY GUY

Photostories

Introduction

My Guy was the first teenage girls' magazine in Britain to use photo-stories. On 4th of March 1978 IPC Magazines launched *My Guy* to supplement its other regular teen titles; *Pink, Mates, Fab 208* and *Oh Boy*. Photostrips were an instant success and soon every teenage magazine had to have them. *Jackie* and *Blue Jeans* from rival firm D.C. Thompson lumbered on with drawn strip for a while but eventually they succumbed to including photostories, too.

It's surprising they came to the UK so late when they'd been around since the 1960s – Monty Python's Terry Gilliam experimented with them in the States before he moved to London, and in Italy they were big business from the early 70s. The Italians would publish long-winded romances – the men dressed in sharp suits and looking impossibly handsome and the women looking like younger versions of Sophia Loren (though the really odd thing was that nobody ever opened their mouth to speak).

My Guy's photostories at first were more about entertainment than reader involvement. Each week there was a five-page complete story, a three-page serial and a two-page photoproblem. With

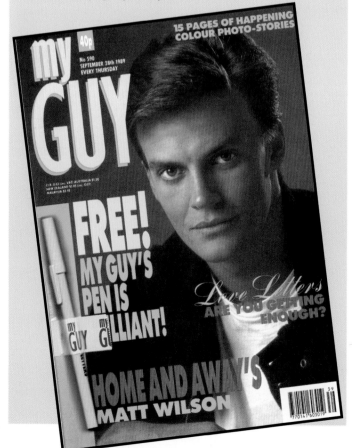

nine frames to the page writers had to construct a story and end it – ideally with a twist – in 40 exchanges of dialogue. They could be romantic, mysterious, quirky, funny and often full of schlock horror. I joined the magazine as a photo-story writer in 1980 and there was far more emphasis on working out a good dramatic story than showing average teenagers doing average teenage stuff. We would steal from anywhere – film plots, TV plots, adverts, even song lyrics. Kate Bush's *Babooshka* single (about a girl dressing up as someone else to tempt her boyfriend) was the perfect photo-story plot on a plate. The things we would steal most frequently would be endings, because you couldn't have the same ending every week.

Love stories were about finding it really difficult to fall in love, then finally doing it – or alternatively – falling in love, then getting separated and then getting back together again. Running-away-from-home stories always ended with the runaway coming home. It couldn't be any other way. The second you departed from the moralistic norm there would be someone blaming teenage girls' magazines for single parent mothers, teenage smoking, an increase in sexually transmitted diseases and truancy. Once we were the reason why not enough girls were taking science GCSEs.

As time went on the formats changed and the scope of the stories narrowed. From the early 80s the stories were almost entirely about the consequences of girls going out with boys and the dressing up box had to go. *My Guy* inherited the *Sisters* photosoap from *Heartbeat* magazine and then started one of its own, *Clare* with a regular cast of characters based around actress Maria Williams who played the eponymous heroine. *Clare* morphed into *Clare – Away from Home*. That was joined by the school soap *Saintbridge* photographed near

Getting the spacing just right between "pen" and "is" was very tricky for this 1989 give-away. When it appeared in print the publisher, Jackie Newcombe, stomped through the door and said, "I know you did it deliberately and I don't think it's very funny."

Twyford and succeeded by the Sixth form college drama *Kingsbrook* photographed at Henley College until the mid-90s. Though none of the long-running stories could be included in this compilation, a lot of the regular cast of *Kingsbrook* turn up in the one-off *Autumn Bay* on page 180 and *Away From Home*'s 'Bradley' pilots the river cruiser on page 134.

Photo-story models came from a variety of sources. Hemma and Michael Sullivan set up an agency called Photopix, supplying models to as many as nine photostory magazines at one time. They were responsible for recruiting students from the London drama schools along with TV extras looking for additional work. The inappropriately named 'Starnest' in North London provided many young hopefuls, while Wendy Milligan revelled in the opportunity to chat up "nice young men" on the streets of Twyford and marshalled the casts of *Away From Home*, *Saintbridge* and *Kingsbrook* for many years. We would also rope in friends, relations and occasionally passers by.

Along with the boys and girls from next door there are a variety of well-known faces in *My Guy: The Photostories*. Some acted in photostories after they had become famous and we had to pay them lots of money for the privilege – Les Hill from *Home & Away*, Scott Michaelson from *Neighbours* and Declan Donnelly of *Byker Grove* fall into that bracket. Others, such as Hugh Grant, Sally Whittaker, Tracey Ullman and Alex Kingston were drama students. N-Sync were unheard of in the UK and their PR, Caroline Norman, persuaded us to run a three-page photostory with the boys. They were suitably bemused by the whole process.

There's a couple of famous *My Guy* fashion models included in this compilation, too. Cat Deeley and BBC Radio One's Sara Cox modelled in several fashion shoots in the early 90s. Cat was picked because she was the perfect age for the readership as she was just starting out in the model business. Sara was chosen because the editor fancied her and would spend ages on the lightbox saying, "I really should get out to a photo shoot," but never did. There's also a couple of WAGs, Alex Pursey (*When the Wind Blows*) married George Best to become Alex Best, while Suzanne Howard (*Best Kept Secret*) married goalkeeper Ian Walker to become Suzi Walker. Touchingly, in the story her boyfriend's called Ian.

Watch out for a special appearance; the hands holding the supposedly death-delivering snake on page 145 are mine. We shot *Murder By Numbers* in the winter of 1980 and kept the snake – inactive because of the cold – in a bag out in the photographer's car till it was needed. The model took one look, went into hysterics and refused to touch it; the most she would do was hold it on the end of a stick. So I had to put on her jacket and threaten Annabel Giles. We put it back in the car and it curled up asleep in its bag on the back seat and was forgotten about. On the way back to London with the heater full on, though, the snake warmed up and began to examine the warm leg that was sat next to it. It was the only time I've ever seen a model glued to the roof of a BMW Five series.

Frank Hopkinson

introducing N Sync

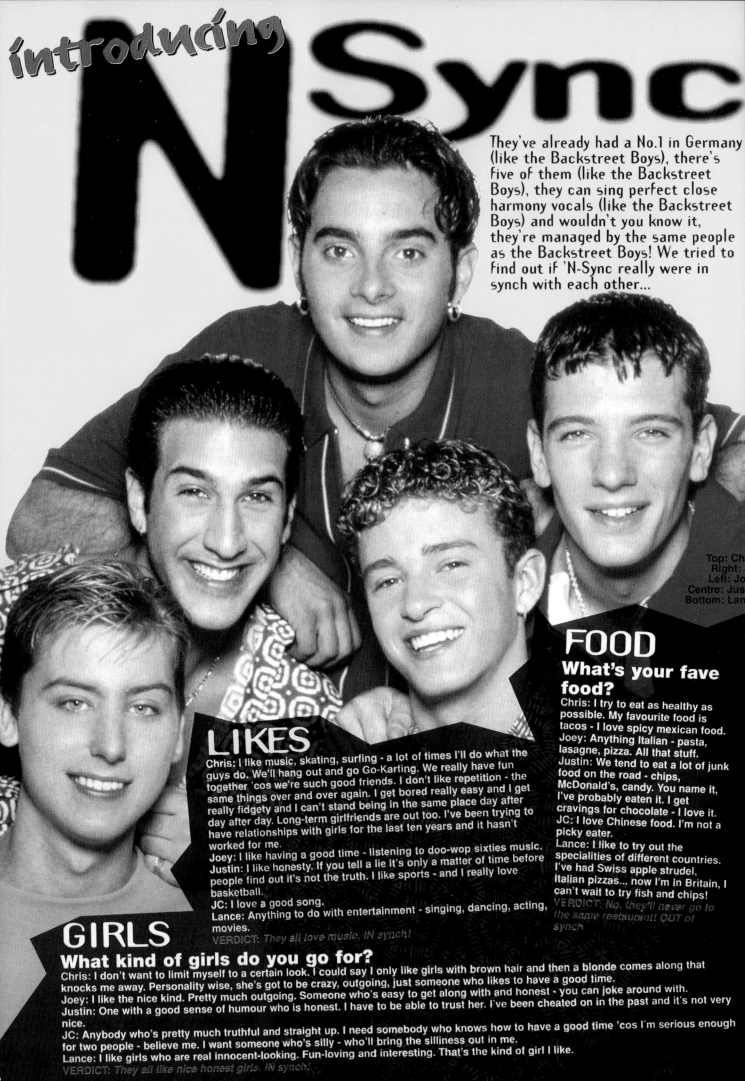

They've already had a No.1 in Germany (like the Backstreet Boys), there's five of them (like the Backstreet Boys), they can sing perfect close harmony vocals (like the Backstreet Boys) and wouldn't you know it, they're managed by the same people as the Backstreet Boys! We tried to find out if 'N-Sync really were in synch with each other...

Top: Chr
Right: J
Left: Joe
Centre: Just
Bottom: Lanc

LIKES

Chris: I like music, skating, surfing - a lot of times I'll do what the guys do. We'll hang out and go Go-Karting. We really have fun together 'cos we're such good friends. I don't like repetition - the same things over and over again. I get bored really easy and I get really fidgety and I can't stand being in the same place day after day after day. Long-term girlfriends are out too. I've been trying to have relationships with girls for the last ten years and it hasn't worked for me.
Joey: I like having a good time - listening to doo-wop sixties music.
Justin: I like honesty. If you tell a lie it's only a matter of time before people find out it's not the truth. I like sports - and I really love basketball.
JC: I love a good song.
Lance: Anything to do with entertainment - singing, dancing, acting, movies.
VERDICT: They all love music. IN synch!

FOOD
What's your fave food?

Chris: I try to eat as healthy as possible. My favourite food is tacos - I love spicy mexican food.
Joey: Anything Italian - pasta, lasagne, pizza. All that stuff.
Justin: We tend to eat a lot of junk food on the road - chips, McDonald's, candy. You name it, I've probably eaten it. I get cravings for chocolate - I love it.
JC: I love Chinese food. I'm not a picky eater.
Lance: I like to try out the specialities of different countries. I've had Swiss apple strudel, Italian pizzas... now I'm in Britain, I can't wait to try fish and chips!
VERDICT: No, they'll never go to the same restaurant! OUT of synch!

GIRLS
What kind of girls do you go for?

Chris: I don't want to limit myself to a certain look. I could say I only like girls with brown hair and then a blonde comes along that knocks me away. Personality wise, she's got to be crazy, outgoing, just someone who likes to have a good time.
Joey: I like the nice kind. Pretty much outgoing. Someone who's easy to get along with and honest - you can joke around with.
Justin: One with a good sense of humour who is honest. I have to be able to trust her. I've been cheated on in the past and it's not very nice.
JC: Anybody who's pretty much truthful and straight up. I need somebody who knows how to have a good time 'cos I'm serious enough for two people - believe me. I want someone who's silly - who'll bring the silliness out in me.
Lance: I like girls who are real innocent-looking. Fun-loving and interesting. That's the kind of girl I like.
VERDICT: They all like nice honest girls. IN synch!

a TWIST in the TALE...

11

A FOOL FOR HIS LOVE!

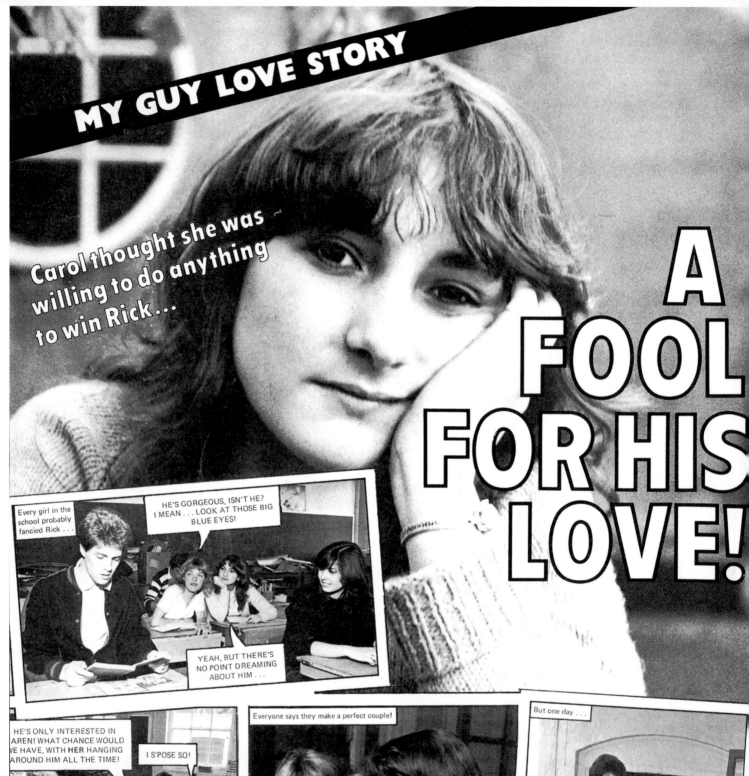

Carol thought she was willing to do anything to win Rick...

Every girl in the school probably fancied Rick...

HE'S GORGEOUS, ISN'T HE? I MEAN... LOOK AT THOSE BIG BLUE EYES!

YEAH, BUT THERE'S NO POINT DREAMING ABOUT HIM...

HE'S ONLY INTERESTED IN KAREN! WHAT CHANCE WOULD WE HAVE, WITH **HER** HANGING AROUND HIM ALL THE TIME!

I S'POSE SO!

Everyone says they make a perfect couple!

I WONDER WHAT IT'S LIKE... TO HAVE SOMEONE SPECIAL LIKE THAT?

'Course I never thought I'd find out...

But one day...

CAROL! I'VE BEEN LOOKING FOR YOU... WOULD YOU MEET ME AFTER CLASS? I'D LIKE TO TALK TO YOU!

M-ME? YES, OF COURSE! BUT...

12

IT'S NOT CHEATING! JUST . . . BEING GOOD FRIENDS!

I DON'T KNOW, RICK. I'VE NEVER DONE ANYTHING LIKE THIS BEFORE.

BUT IF IT MEANS YOU'LL LIKE ME, I'LL DO IT!

So . . .

. . . I helped him cheat in the exams . . .

And although I was still mad about Rick . . .

IT MUST BE GREAT BEING RICK'S GIRLFRIEND, CAROL! YOU'RE SO LUCKY!

. . . I felt bad about the cheating!

WHY DON'T YOU SHUT UP ABOUT ME AND RICK! JUST LEAVE ME ALONE!

BUT CAROL—!?

. . . and Rick's words kept echoing in my head . . .

"Only using Carol . . . not interest in her . . .!"

I wanted to get away to be on my own, but —

. . . SO YOU SEE, KAREN, IT'S **YOU** I REALLY WANT! I'M ONLY USING CAROL TO GET THROUGH MY EXAMS! YOU DON'T THINK I'D BE INTERESTED IN **HER**, DO YOU?

WELL, I MUST ADMIT, YOU HAD ME WORRIED!

BUT WHAT AM I GOING TO DO? RICK'LL EXPECT ME TO HELP HIM IN THE END OF TERM EXAM TOMORROW! OH, I'VE BEEN SUCH A FOOL!

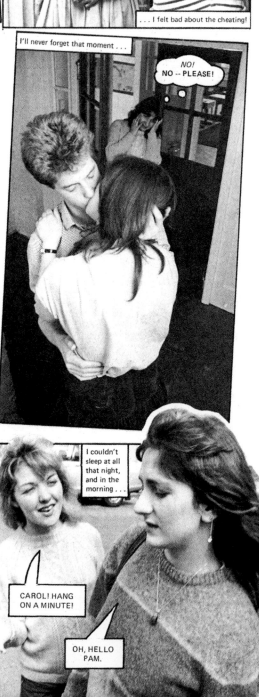

I'll never forget that moment . . .

NO! NO -- PLEASE!

I couldn't sleep at all that night, and in the morning . . .

CAROL! HANG ON A MINUTE!

OH, HELLO PAM.

LISTEN, I'M SORRY I SHOUTED AT YOU LIKE THAT YESTERDAY, PAM! I DIDN'T MEAN IT!

THAT'S OKAY, CAROL! I GUESS YOU'VE GOT SOMETHING ON YOUR MIND THESE DAYS.

IT'S JUST THIS EXAM TODAY, IT'S AN IMPORTANT ONE, IT MEANS A LOT TO RICK, HE'S A BIT WORRIED ABOUT IT!

Rick was waiting for me in the exam room . . .

HEY, CAROL! COME AND SIT OVER HERE!

NO, I DON'T THINK SO, RICK . . .

I'd made my decision . . .

. . . I wasn't going to be used by Rick again!

And on the last day of term . . .

WELL DONE, CAROL! I'M REALLY PROUD OF YOU! IMAGINE BEING MADE CLASS CAPTAIN!

THANKS, PAM! IT WAS A SURPRISE TO ME TOO!

But there was someone who wasn't pleased for me --

WELL, I'LL SEE YOU TOMORROW THEN. 'BYE CAROL!

Rick hadn't spoken to me again!

BUT I GUESS I CAN LIVE WITH IT NOW!

And there were other things to think about too . . .

HEY, CAROL! CONGRATULATIONS ON GETTING MADE SCHOOL CAPTAIN!

THANKS, IAN.

WHAT KIND OF THINGS DO SCHOOL CAPTAINS DO OUT OF SCHOOL?

OH, ALL KINDS! NOTHING SERIOUS — JUST FUN, AND MESSING ABOUT — AND ROMANCE!

You know what they say — all work and no play . . .

. . . is a big mistake!

MY GUY
THE END

15

TOY BOY

Did Damian really stand a chance with a 20-year-old girl...?

OOOHHWW! GO IN!

SHE'S WORTH A SMALL DETOUR.

HAVING TROUBLE?

NO, I REALLY LOVE TALKING TO MACHINES.

I COULD DO THAT, NO PROBLEMS

I BET YOU COULD.

Continued on page 50

18

The time for smiling was over, the time for screaming about to begin!

MURDER BY NUMBERS

AT LAST, A CHANCE TO READ THE NEWSPAPER AND RELAX. I'VE BEEN LOOKING FORWARD TO THIS FOR A LONG TIME.

I'LL TAKE THE PHONE OFF THE HOOK TOMORROW. THE LAST THING I WANT IS MY AGENT RINGING ME UP.

But suddenly, in the paper. . .

GIRL KILLED IN GAS EXPLOSION!

WHY DON'T THEY GET ON WITH IT, I'M FED UP OF WAITING ROUND HERE!

I REMEMBER THAT FACE, I WONDER WHY?

OF COURSE SHE WAS IN THE BEAUTY CONTEST, THAT MUST HAVE BEEN TWO YEARS AGO NOW. I REMEMBER ELLEN, SHE WAS REALLY STRUNG UP, THE NIGHT OF THE COMPETITION, SHE PUT EVERYBODY ON EDGE.

TAKE IT EASY, WE'VE STILL GOT HALF AN HOUR TO GO, YOU SHOULDN'T HAVE GOT CHANGED SO EARLY.

I DON'T KNOW WHAT IT'S GOING TO BE LIKE WHEN THE COMPETITION STARTS, BUT YOU CAN FEEL THE TENSION ALREADY.

WHO D'YOU THINK'S GOING TO WIN, THAT BLACK GIRL LOOKS PRETTY.

I DON'T KNOW, IT'S MORE A QUESTION OF LUCK I THINK. ANYWAY I'VE TAKEN MY CONTACT LENSES OUT, I CAN'T SEE ANYBODY PROPERLY.

OH NO, I'VE FORGOTTEN WHAT I WAS GOING TO SAY TO THE COMPERE.

IT'S TOO LATE NOW, TELL HIM THE FIRST THING THAT COMES INTO YOUR HEAD.

The competition started and it was all smiles for the judges and the cameras and the specially invited audience.

MADELINE GRAY COMES FROM SEVENOAKS, SHE'S 23 AND SHE WORKS IN AN ESTATE AGENT'S. I BET THERE ARE A LOT OF FELLAS WHO'D LIKE TO GET THEIR HANDS ON HER PROPERTY.

Then there were the interviews. . .

SHE'S A BIG GIRL TOO, SO IF THERE ARE ANY BASKETBALL TEAMS LOOKING IN!

I LOVE TO TAKE A LONG HOT BATH.

IF YOU EVER WANT SOMEONE TO SCRUB YOUR BACK, I'LL GIVE YOU MY PHONE NUMBER.

WHAT'S YOUR FAVOURITE HOBBY?

I'M VERY FOND OF ANIMALS. I LOVE LOOKING AFTER PETS.

INTERESTED IN BODY BUILDING AND GYMNASTICS, SHE LOOKS LIKE A NICE STRONG GIRL!

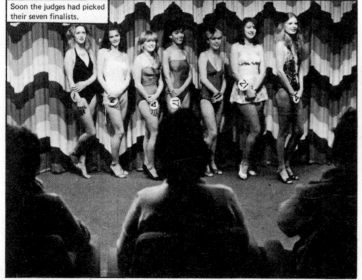

Soon the judges had picked their seven finalists.

All that was left was the decision.

AND IN FIFTH PLACE, ELLEN DANIELS FROM COVENTRY!

"You've won! You're a star!"

BUT THE WINNER IS ALISON WILLIAMS FROM CARDIFF!

It was an emotional moment, Alison had won!

As she started on the traditional winner's parade, the tears began to flow.

It was a night she'd never forget.

YOU'VE WON! YOU'RE A STAR!

I OUGHT TO GO AND SEE JUDY, I HAVEN'T SEEN HER FOR MONTHS.

THERE ISN'T A LIGHT ON IN THE HOUSE, I HOPE SHE'S IN, I HAVEN'T TOLD HER I'M COMING.

THE FRONT DOOR WAS WIDE OPEN, BUT THERE DOESN'T SEEM TO BE ANYONE IN.

JUDY! WHERE ARE YOU?

OH MY GOD!

Judy was dead!

MY GUY

Continued on Page 53

21

Outside.

AND I THOUGHT YOU SAID **LAST WEEK'S** RACE WAS IMPORTANT, TOO.

IT WAS, IT'S PART OF THE SUMMER SERIES. THERE'S EIGHT RACES AND THEY COUNT YOUR BEST SEVEN. I'VE GOT ANOTHER THREE TO GO.

'COURSE YOU DON'T. YOU CAN COME DOWN AND WATCH IF YOU WANT.

YOU SPEND SO MUCH TIME AT THE SAILING CLUB AS IT IS – FIXING SAILS, PAINTING THE HULL, I GET THE FEELING I TAKE SECOND PLACE TO THE BOAT. . .SORRY, THE DINGHY.

NO THANKS, I DON'T WANT TO SPEND MY SUNDAY AFTERNOONS TALKING ABOUT SPLICING THE MAINBRACE.

WISH ME LUCK.

YEAH, GOOD LUCK.

. IF I'VE GOT ANY LUCK AT ALL. THEY'LL CANCEL THE RACE THROUGH LACK OF WIND.

ACTUALLY IT'S NOT SO BAD BEING ON MY OWN ON A SUNDAY AFTERNOON. IF ROGER WAS HERE HE'D ONLY BE FIDGETING TO DO SOMETHING.

AT LEAST THIS WAY I GET TO RELAX.

A couple of hours later.

I CAN'T STAND MUCH MORE OF THIS SUN. TALK ABOUT HAVING TOO MUCH OF A GOOD THING.

Natalie went down to the sailing club to find Roger.

I WONDER WHICH ONE IS HIS? HE DID TELL ME THE SAIL NUMBER.

THAT'S ROGER'S – IT'S CALLED 'WINCHAT' OR SOMETHING LIKE THAT.

But then Natalie saw something she wasn't expecting.

COME ON, YOU COULD GET UP THERE YOURSELF EASILY!

23

25

Natalie knew there was no way she could hold on to Roger — it was all hopeless.

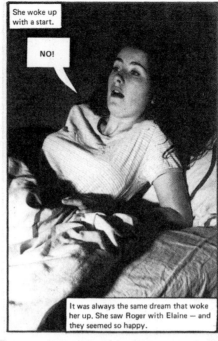

She woke up with a start.

NO!

It was always the same dream that woke her up. She saw Roger with Elaine — and they seemed so happy.

Natalie couldn't sleep any more.

THIS IS A STUPID WAY TO GO ON. MAYBE IF I TALKED TO HER ABOUT IT, TOLD HER HOW MUCH I CARE FOR ROGER...

So that Sunday.

ROGER DIDN'T EVEN MENTION THE SAILING CLUB THIS WEEK SO I KNOW HE DOESN'T WANT ME TO CALL BY.

I HOPE HE DOESN'T SEE ME HERE. HE'LL JUST THINK I'M PLAYING THE JEALOUS GIRLFRIEND. IT'S A RISK I'VE GOT TO TAKE.

THERE SHE IS. HMM, I DIDN'T THINK ROGER WENT FOR HER TYPE. LET'S SEE HOW SHE REACTS WHEN I BREAK THE NEWS TO HER. THAT SHE'S BEING TWO-TIMED.

YOU MUST BE ELAINE.

THAT'S RIGHT.

IT'S ALRIGHT, YOU DON'T KNOW ME.

YOU'RE NATALIE.

YES, YES I AM. HOW DID YOU KNOW THAT?

ROGER'S ALWAYS TALKING ABOUT YOU. HE SHOWED ME A PHOTO TOO.

EXCUSE ME, I'VE GOT TO TIGHTEN THE HALYARD, IT'S A BIT LOOSE. DID HE TELL YOU ABOUT LAST SUNDAY?

NO, HE DOESN'T SAY MUCH ABOUT HIS SAILING.

OH, I WISH HE HAD.

I WISH HE HAD, TOO.

26

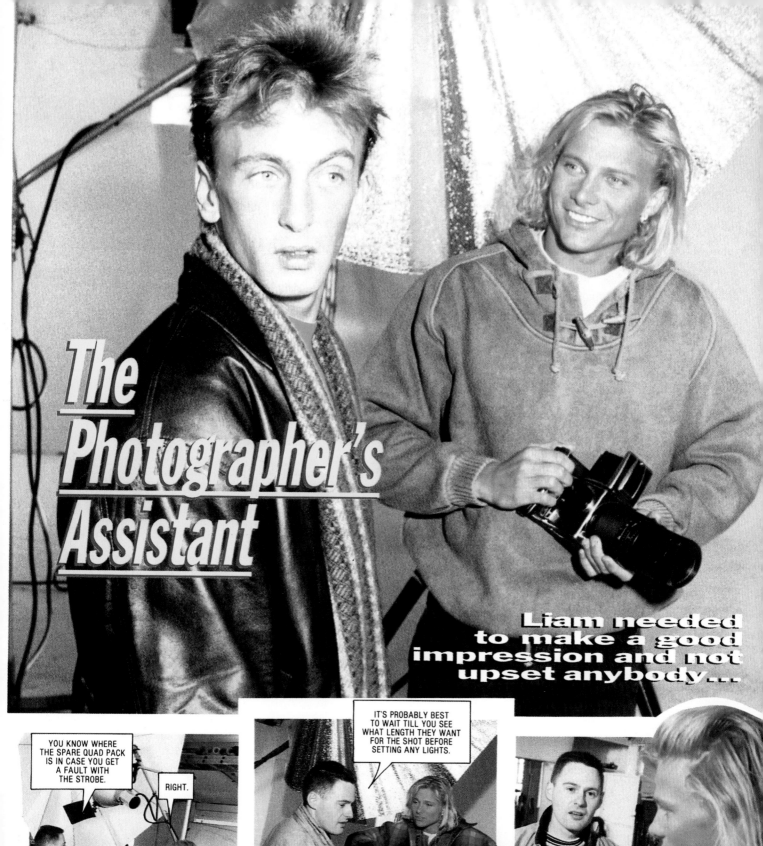

The Photographer's Assistant

Liam needed to make a good impression and not upset anybody...

30

Continued on page 74

31

MY GUY PROBLEM STORY

SHE WON'T

Name: Kim Penman

Problem: Kim's under threat from her guy ex-girlfriend—and it could split them u[...]

When I started going out with Derek I was really excited.

OH BEV, I JUST COULDN'T BELIEVE IT WHEN DEREK ASKED ME OUT! I'VE FANCIED HIM FOR AGES, BUT I THOUGHT THINGS WERE SERIOUS BETWEEN HIM AND MARYLIN, SO I TOOK IT FOR GRANTED THAT HE WOULDN'T TAKE ME OUT.

WELL I DON'T WANT TO WORRY YOU, BUT I OVERHEARD MARYLIN TALKING TO ONE OF HER MATES – SHE STILL FANCIES HIM.

WELL SO WHAT? DEREK FINISHED WITH HER AND FROM WHAT HE TOLD ME IT SEEMS LIKE FOR GOOD.

Derek told me things had been bad between them for a long time, so my conscience was clear.

WELL WHAT DO YOU WANT TO DO TONIGHT?

WE COULD GO TO SEE *ARTHUR* IT'S SUPPOSED TO BE A GREAT FILM.

Things between us were so good . . .

THAT'S FINE BY ME. I'LL PICK YOU UP AROUND SEVEN THEN.

I'LL BE READY AND WAITING!

. . . and I knew that it wouldn't be long before he asked me to go steady.

But as soon as Derek had gone.

M-MARYLIN, I DIDN'T SEE YOU THERE. I . . .

I BET YOU DIDN'T. WELL YOU'RE GOING TO BE SEEING A LOT OF ME FROM NOW ON. YOU SEE I WANT DEREK BACK AND YOU'RE THE PERSON WHO'S COME BETWEEN US. IF YOU KNOW WHAT'S GOOD FOR YOU YOU'LL LEAVE HIM ALONE.

WAIT, MARYLIN . . .

. . . IT'S UP TO YOU. EITHER YOU DITCH DEREK OR YOU COULD FIND THAT THINGS ARE GOING TO GET VERY UNPLEASANT. SUIT YOURSELF.

I felt numb as she walked away. Some of the things she had said just weren't true.

I thought about nothing else for the next few days.

MAYBE I'M WORRYING ABOUT NOTHING. MARYLIN'S GOT A LOT OF TOUGH FRIENDS, BUT SURELY SHE WOULDN'T . . .? NO, SHE'S JUST TRYING TO SCARE ME. SHE MUST KNOW THAT DEREK DOESN'T FANCY HER ANY MORE. HER PRIDE'S BEEN HURT, THAT'S ALL.

But then something happened that made me change my mind.

HEY WATCH IT, YOU COULD HAVE KNOCKED ME OVER!

YOU'RE LUCKY THAT I DIDN'T. NEXT TIME YOU WON'T BE SO LUCKY. BUT IF YOU CHUCKED DEREK I'D BE MUCH MORE CAREFUL, DO YOU GET MY MEANING?

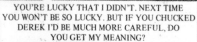

I suddenly realised! Marilyn had put her up to it.

They were always hanging around, making me feel uncomfortable.

WHY IS SHE DOING THIS TO ME? I DIDN'T STEAL DEREK AWAY FROM HER – BUT I CAN'T TELL HIM WHAT SHE'S DOING HE'LL JUST THINK I'M BITCHING.

THE HELP PAGES

LET HIM BE MINE!

I was so worried even Derek noticed the change in me.

I'M SORRY I HAVEN'T BEEN MUCH FUN TONIGHT DEREK, IT'S JUST THAT I'M FEELING A BIT OFF COLOUR.

I WONDERED WHAT WAS WRONG, YOU HAVEN'T BEEN YOURSELF FOR A FEW DAYS.

I hated lying to him, but what else could I do?

I began to dread going to school.

I CAN'T STAND THE WAY SHE KEEPS WATCHING ME! I CAN'T MAKE DEREK STOP LIKING ME, WHY CAN'T SHE SEE THAT?

Marylin watched my every move.

IT'S NO GOOD RUNNING AWAY KIM! AND I'M GETTING TIRED OF WAITING FOR YOU TO MAKE YOUR MIND UP. DON'T THINK I'M GOING TO GO AWAY AND FORGET WHAT YOU'VE DONE – I WON'T.

LEAVE ME ALONE MARYLIN, PLEASE LEAVE ME ALONE!

I was really scared and it showed.

It was the worst mistake I could've made.

I'M NEVER GOING TO LEAVE YOU ALONE! SO LONG AS YOU'VE GOT DEREK, NEVER!

LET GO MARYLIN, PLEASE LET GO. YOU'RE HURTING ME!

Now she knew how scared I was she wouldn't give up!

OH CHRIS, WHAT AM I GOING TO DO? I REALLY WANT TO KEEP GOING OUT WITH DEREK, BUT IF I DON'T GIVE HIM UP THERE'S NO TELLING WHAT MARYLIN WILL DO.

Unfortunately being bullied is something most people have to face at some time. Even though you're in no way to blame for their break-up, Marylin still feels bitter and rejected. She can't take it out on Derek, so she's taking it out on you; you've become the focus for her anger. Once she's got over losing him and realises that he won't be coming back she'll understand that there's no point in bothering and bullying you. But until that time there's no reason why you should suffer. Stop feeling scared and share your fears with people who can help, and they'll make sure she leaves you alone. And don't put off telling people what's going on any longer.

Chris gives her advice

You must tell Derek what's been going on right away.

... SO YOU SEE SHE THINKS IF SHE THREATENS ME I'LL GIVE YOU UP. I'M SO SCARED DEREK.

WE CAN'T LET HER GET AWAY WITH THIS. IF SHE SEES THAT WE'RE NOT GOING TO SPLIT UP, MAYBE SHE'LL LEAVE YOU ALONE.

Sharing your fears won't make them go away, but at least you'll have Derek's support.

And Marilyn will realise that you have no intention of giving him up. . .

... SO YOU SEE YOU'RE WASTING YOUR TIME MARYLIN. EVEN IF I WASN'T GOING OUT WITH KIM, WHICH I STILL AM, I WOULDN'T GO OUT WITH YOU AGAIN!

...she may decide to save face and then leave you in peace.

But if she doesn't . . .

YOU SHOULD HAVE COME TO ME BEFORE KIM. BULLYING'S A SERIOUS THING. ANYWAY I'LL HAVE A WORD WITH MARYLIN AND MAKE HER SEE SENSE, SO YOU CAN STOP WORRYING.

A word with your form teacher should put your mind at rest.

When Marylin knows she's going to cause trouble for no-one but herself by her actions. . .

... YES IT'S A GREAT DISCO, DEREK AND I ARE GOING THERE TONIGHT!

... things will soon get back to normal.

MY GUY

TRUE LOVE STORY

Was Andrea's little brother about to ruin her first date...?

35

What dark secrets lay behind closed doors?

THE GIRL WHO CAME TO STAY

Ralph had hired a private detective. . .

HERE'S YOUR CHEQUE MR DAWSON — I'M SURE YOU'LL FIND EVERYTHING IN ORDER!

I'M SURE I WILL, SIR!

. . .to report on his girlfriend.

WELL! YOU'VE CERTAINLY DONE A GOOD JOB — THIS REPORT'S VERY DETAILED!

MMM. . .IT WASN'T VERY DIFFICULT TO FIND OUT ABOUT THE YOUNG LADY, SIR. SHE'S HAD A LOT OF VERY RICH GENTLEMEN FRIENDS AND THEY WERE ALL VERY WILLING TO TALK ABOUT HER.

And, when Ralph was alone. . .

AND TO THINK I FELT GUILTY ABOUT CHECKING UP ON HER! I KNEW IT WAS RISKY MARRYING AN ACTRESS IN THE PUBLIC EYE. . . BUT SHE'S CERTAINLY MADE QUITE A REPUTATION FOR HERSELF!

LOOKING AT THIS MAKES ME THINK THAT SHE REALLY IS AFTER MY MONEY. . .

BUT EVEN IF SHE IS A FORTUNE HUNTER — I STILL LOVE HER AND SHE SAYS SHE LOVES ME. . .SO WHAT DO I DO? I SUPPOSE THERE'S NO HARM IN MAKING SURE, THOUGH. . .

A BEAUTIFUL HOME MADE UGLY BY MADNESS!

THE GIRL WHO CAME TO STAY

The Girl Who Came To Stay was originally published in My Guy as a serial, running over four weeks. Now we've put all four episodes together to make one extra long story.

Would Jenny's ordeal as an unwelcome guest ruin the chance of a lifetime?

B...BUT I CAN'T LEAVE NOW! I'VE COME ALL THIS WAY TO MEET YOU!

DO WHAT YOU LIKE! I DON'T CARE AS LONG AS YOU DON'T STEAL THE SILVER!

WELL, I'M BLOWED IF I'M GOING! SHE CAN'T BE RALPH'S SISTER — I'LL WAIT FOR HIM, HE'LL EXPLAIN!

THERE ARE SOME LOVELY THINGS IN THIS ROOM — THEY MUST BE FAMILY HEIRLOOMS, WORTH A FORTUNE I SHOULD THINK!

IT'S STRANGE, BUT I'M SURE I'VE SEEN THAT GIRL SOMEWHERE BEFORE!

But, suddenly, she was pounced on.

KEEP YOUR DIRTY, THIEVING LITTLE HANDS OFF THAT!

I. . .I'M SORRY! I WAS ONLY LOOKING!

I KNOW YOUR TYPE! BET YOU'RE AN EX CON OR SOMETHING!

BUT I'VE NEVER STOLEN ANYTHING IN MY LIFE — YOU CAN TRUST ME, HONESTLY!

WHERE **HAVE** I SEEN HER BEFORE?

CECIL WILL CERTAINLY HAVE SOMETHING TO SAY ABOUT THIS IF YOU'VE DAMAGED THIS VASE — HE'S **VERY** PARTICULAR, YOU KNOW!

W. . .WHO'S CECIL?

MY HUSBAND OF COURSE! MMM. . .IF I POLISH HARD ENOUGH HE MAY NOT FIND THE FINGER PRINTS. . .YOU **MIGHT** GET AWAY WITH IT THIS TIME!

Jenny waited for Ralph alone. . .

HURRY UP, RALPH — **PLEASE** — DON'T LEAVE ME ALONE WITH A MAD WOMAN!

THE DOOR! THAT MUST BE HIM NOW!

OH, RALPH! I'M **SO** GLAD TO SEE YOU. THERE'S A LOONY HERE WHO CLAIMS TO BE YOUR SISTER — SHE'S A REAL NUTCASE!

SHE'S MAD! AND RALPH DIDN'T MENTION HER HUSBAND!

I'M DISAPPOINTED IN YOU, JENNY! MY SISTER IS MENTALLY ILL. IT'S SOMETHING THAT RUNS IN OUR FAMILY AND SHOULDN'T BE LAUGHED AT!

M. . .MADNESS? RUNS IN YOUR FAMILY? WHAT ABOUT HER HUSBAND?

OF COURSE I DO, RALPH!

NOW, RALPH — YOU SIT IN YOUR USUAL PLACE AND THAT CRIMINAL FRIEND OF YOURS CAN MAKE UP HER OWN MIND WHERE SHE SITS — CECIL'S HERE TO KEEP AN EYE ON HER!

WHY ARE THESE FOUR CUPS — THERE ARE ONLY THREE OF US. . .

HE DOESN'T EXIST! CECIL IS PURELY A FIGMENT OF HER IMAGINATION, I HOPE YOU'LL HUMOUR JESSICA FOR MY SAKE, JENNY. . . IF YOU STILL WANT TO MARRY ME, THAT IS . . .

WELL, I WON'T HAVE TO PUT UP WITH HER FOR LONG, JUST UNTIL WE'RE MARRIED I MIGHT AS WELL TRY. . .

ONE'S FOR CECIL OF COURSE!

THE GIRL WHO CAME TO STAY

Would money tempt Jenny to marry into madness?

When this story first appeared in My Guy several years ago, you had to wait a week from the end of one episode to the start of the next. Fortunately, you don't have to do that now — it's all here in one bumper read!

WHAT AM I GOING TO DO? I CAN'T LIVE HERE WITH JESSICA WHEN RALPH AND I GET MARRIED. I'LL BE STUCK HERE WITH HER EVERY DAY!

AND MADNESS RUNS IN THE FAMILY... WHAT IF WE HAVE CHILDREN, WILL THEY ALL BE LIKE JESSICA?

I SHOULD REALLY FEEL SORRY FOR HER, I SUPPOSE... I OUGHT TO MAKE AN EFFORT, SHE'S PROBABLY FRIGHTENED OF ME!

I'VE GOT TO GET OUT OF THIS PLACE! RALPH CAN'T EXPECT ME TO LIVE WITH A MADWOMAN!

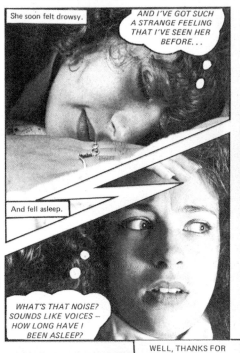

She soon felt drowsy.

AND I'VE GOT SUCH A STRANGE FEELING THAT I'VE SEEN HER BEFORE...

And fell asleep.

WHAT'S THAT NOISE? SOUNDS LIKE VOICES – HOW LONG HAVE I BEEN ASLEEP?

She went quietly downstairs.

THAT SOUNDS LIKE RALPH'S VOICE – I WONDER WHO HE'S TALKING TO?

And, through the crack in the sitting room door...

WHO DO I MAKE THE CHEQUE PAYABLE TO?

OH, USE MY STAGE NAME – SELENA JAMES.

WELL, YOU'VE CERTAINLY HELPED ME OUT. I KNEW JENNY WAS A FORTUNE HUNTER BECAUSE I HAD HER FOLLOWED – I HAD TO FIND OUT IF SHE WAS AFTER MY MONEY...

MMM... SO YOU INVENTED A MAD SISTER TO SEE IF SHE'D BE PUT OFF! YOU'LL SOON FIND OUT IF SHE LOVES YOU OR YOUR MONEY, MR. ST. CLAIRE! I WAS ENOUGH TO PUT ANYONE OFF!

WELL, THANKS FOR EVERYTHING, SELENA! THAT WAS QUITE A PERFORMANCE YOU LAID ON!

I SHOULD BE THANKING YOU! THIS IS THE MOST HIGHLY-PAID JOB I'VE EVER HAD – BEATS THE WINTER SEASON IN BLACKPOOL ANY DAY!

NO! IT CAN'T BE TRUE! HE TRICKED ME!

Jenny overheard the whole conversation.

I KNEW I'D SEEN HER SOMEWHERE BEFORE! SHE WAS IN THE CHORUS OF THAT MUSICAL I DID LAST WINTER!

OH, RALPH! HOW COULD YOU DO SUCH A THING? YOU PUT ME THROUGH ALL THIS BECAUSE YOU THOUGHT I WAS AFTER YOUR MONEY!

MY GUY **TURN OVER FOR THE FINAL GRIPPING CHAPTER!**

45

By now you're probably wondering how people waited a month for the end of this story. Well, you don't have to — get stuck into the last exciting chapter now . . .

And, the next morning. . .

I STILL CAN'T BELIEVE HE TRICKED ME!

. . . Jenny went down to breakfast.

She hadn't slept a wink. . .

HI, JENNY! SLEEP WELL?

MMM! WHERE'S JESSICA?

. . . but she didn't tell Ralph.

THE GIRL WHO CAME TO STAY

The cruel joke was over, but who would have the last laugh?

SHE ER WENT TO STAY WITH OUR AUNT FOR A WHILE. . .

WHAT A BARE-FACED LIE! HE'S PAID HER OFF!

OH, WHAT A SHAME! I REALLY LIKED HER!

YOU DID? WHAT ABOUT HER . . . ER — PROBLEM?

I FEEL SORRY FOR HER, RALPH! I'D LIKE TO HELP HER!

Jenny knew there was no danger of Jessica returning . . .

SHE'S YOUR SISTER, AND I'LL DO MY BEST TO MAKE HER HAPPY BECAUSE I LOVE **YOU**!

YOU DON'T KNOW HOW MUCH THIS MEANS TO ME — THE FACT THAT YOU'RE STILL WILLING TO MARRY ME — EVEN THOUGH THERE'S MADNESS IN THE FAMILY!

. . . because she knew that Ralph had tricked her.

But she played along with the game . . .

AND TO THINK I EVER DOUBTED YOU! YOU LOVE ME — IN SPITE OF EVERY-THING!

OH, YES! I KNOW **EXACTLY** WHAT I'M LETTING MYSELF IN FOR!

. . . but this time. . .

LET'S GET MARRIED STRAIGHT AWAY, RALPH — **TODAY**!

. . . she had the winning hand.

TODAY? BUT DARLING, ARE YOU SURE? NO ONE WOULD MARRY US AT SUCH SHORT NOTICE — SURELY!

I KNOW SOMEONE WHO WOULD! MY FLATMATE'S BROTHER'S A VICAR — I'LL PHONE HIM!

Now he **knew** she wasn't after his money.

And, that afternoon. . .

STILL WANT TO GO THROUGH WITH IT? YOU HAVEN'T CHANGED YOUR MIND, HAVE YOU?

OF COURSE NOT! I KNOW EXACTLY WHAT I'M DOING!

Ralph looked at Jenny lovingly. . .

. . . as he slipped the ring on to her finger.

THANK YOU SO MUCH!

YES, I'M SORRY YOU HAD TO BE DRAGGED OUT AT SUCH SHORT NOTICE!

THINK NOTHING OF IT! IT'S A PLEASURE DOING A FAVOUR FOR AN OLD FRIEND LIKE JENNY!

FROCK
till you drop

With as
much
Christmas
presence as
this – you
can certainly
make a party

Frocks on the Cox

Radio One's Sara Cox was a regular My Guy fashion model in the early nineties. Highlights of her modelling for the magazine included fishing on Battersea common, wearing posh frocks for a Christmas feature and stroking a silver phalus in docklands.

Silver

O Short sleeve silver dress:
Miss Selfridge £34.99
Turban made from tights:
Pamela Mann £9.99 (Tel: 0455 636231)
O White shimmery top: Top Shop £16.99
Silver slip: Miss Selfridge £26.99

O White T-shirt with silver star:
Miss Selfridge £14.99
Silver mini skirt: Miss Selfridge £12.99
O Bikini top: Miss Selfridge £19.99
Silver fitted jacket: Zack £39.99 (Tel: 071-580 9512)
Silver mini skirt: Zack £14.99 as above

Worn throughout: Silver DMs: Shellys
£44.99 - Silver lace-ups: Snob £24.99 -
Photographer: Mike Prior - Styling: Nikki
Herridge - Hair and make-up: Tinks Reding

...races, dungarees and
...rts are all angling for
...this summer

Brown vest: River
Island £3.99
Cream grandad
shirt: Freemans
(GM81664) £37.99
Floral skirt: River
Island £19.99
Hat: Racing Green
£10.00

Fishing.

Cream top: Freemans
(WXD5391) £12.99
Green padded
waistcoat: Freemans
(WPO575) £29.99
Jeans: Model's own
Hat: Racing Green
£10.00

Story Update: Damian couldn't believe his luck, chatting up 'an older woman'. But it looks like his luck has run out . . .

TOY BOY

I S'POSE I HAVE TO PUT IT DOWN TO EXPERIENCE.

WHAT WOULD I SAY TO HER NEXT TIME. . ?

Damian couldn't believe his luck

But then something interesting happened.

OI, YOU'RE NOT GOING TO GIVE UP **THAT** EASILY ARE YOU?

IT'S MY BIRTHDAY.

50

Continued on page 84

MURDER BY NUMBERS

They started with five finalists - now there were only three!

Back at the C.I.D.

I KNOW IT'S DISTRESSING MISS WILLIAMS BUT IF I COULD ASK YOU SOME QUESTIONS, WE CAN SORT THIS THING OUT.

HOW LONG HAD YOU KNOWN THE DECEASED?

TWO YEARS, I HARDLY KNEW HER THOUGH, WE MET AT A BEAUTY CONTEST.

DID YOU KEEP IN CLOSE CONTACT?

NO, I'VE SEEN JUDY ON AND OFF OVER THE PAST TWO YEARS BUT WE NEVER HAD MUCH TIME TO TALK.

WE'VE BOTH BEEN QUITE SUCCESSFUL SINCE THE COMPETITION. I STARTED OFF IN MODELLING AND MOVED UP TO TELEVISION WORK. SHE BOUGHT HER OWN DRESS SHOP AND WENT INTO BUSINESS.

WHEN YOU SPOKE TO HER ON THE PHONE DID SHE SEEM ANXIOUS?

I DIDN'T SPEAK TO HER, I JUST TURNED UP ON THE SPUR OF THE MOMENT. IT WAS GOING TO BE A SURPRISE.

WHAT MADE YOU GO AND VISIT HER OUT OF THE BLUE.

ELLEN, IT WAS ELLEN DANIELS, THE GIRL THAT WAS KILLED IN THAT HOUSE EXPLOSION. SHE WAS IN THE BEAUTY CONTEST TOO. I SAW IT IN THE PAPER AND IT REMINDED ME.

SHE WAS IN THE CONTEST TOO? THAT'S VERY IMPORTANT, VERY IMPORTANT INDEED.

At Alison's house.

THESE ARE THE PHOTOS FROM THE CONTEST, YOU WON'T FIND EVERYONE THERE, BUT BOTH ELLEN AND JUDY ARE THERE.

The first photo showed the winners of the competition

SO YOU WON IT?

I'M AFRAID SO.

I CAN SEE JUDY, WHICH ONE IS ELLEN?

GIVE IT TO ME A SECOND.

THAT'S ELLEN THERE.

AND ELLEN WAS FIFTH AND JUDY WAS FOURTH?

THAT'S RIGHT.

WHAT IF ELLEN'S DEATH WASN'T AN ACCIDENT. THAT LEAVES US WITH TWO MURDERED BEAUTY QUEENS FROM THE SAME COMPETITION.

WHAT ARE YOU TRYING TO SAY?

IT'S TOO MUCH OF A COINCIDENCE COMING SO CLOSE TOGETHER. I'VE GOT TO INVESTIGATE EVERY POSSIBILITY AND THIS IS ONE I CAN'T IGNORE.

THAT SOMEONE HAS A GRUDGE?

REVENGE IS THE ONLY MOTIVE I CAN THINK OF AT THE MOMENT, BUT TWO YEARS IS A LONG TIME TO WAIT FOR REVENGE.

Next day...

...I'M TRYING TO GET IN TOUCH WITH YOUR WIFE, IT'S PURELY A ROUTINE MATTER, WE'RE TRYING TO GET IN TOUCH WITH EVERYONE WHO WAS IN A BEAUTY COMPETITION TWO YEARS AGO.

I'M SORRY OFFICER, SHE'LL BE AT HER HEALTH CLUB TODAY, I HAVEN'T GOT THE NUMBER.

NOT TO WORRY SIR, I'LL CONTACT HER THIS EVENING, IT SHOULD BE ALL RIGHT.

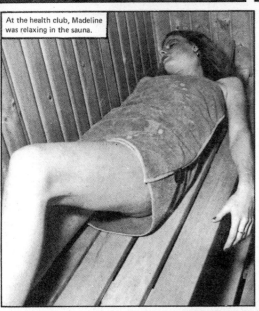

At the health club, Madeline was relaxing in the sauna.

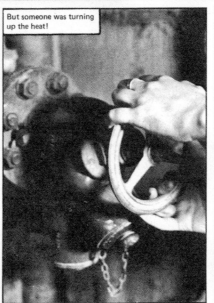

But someone was turning up the heat!

I MUST GO FOR A SHOWER, IT'S GETTING TOO HOT IN HERE — I FEEL AS THOUGH I'M GOING TO SUFFOCATE.

SOMEONE'S LOCKED THE DOOR I CAN'T GET IT OPEN!

HEY! OPEN THE DOOR, I'M CHOKING IN HERE! OPEN THE DOOR!

But there was no one around to help.

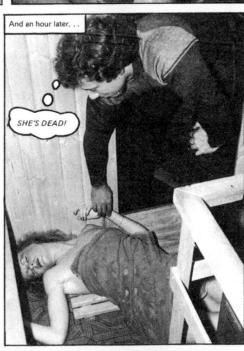

And an hour later...

SHE'S DEAD!

MY GUY

Continued on Page 87

55

GIVING WAY

Grace wouldn't abandon her bike for anything or anyone

YOU COULD HAVE DONE IT YOURSELF, IT'S ONLY 'COS I'VE GOT A WORKSHOP MANUAL AND I'VE DONE IT BEFORE.

TRY IT NOW AND SEE WHAT HAPPENS.

FINGERS CROSSED.

HEY, IT STARTED FIRST TIME! YOU'RE A GENIUS.

YEAH? JUST WAIT FOR THE PLUGS TO OIL UP ONE MORNING WHEN YOU'RE LATE. THEN YOU WON'T BE SO EXCITED.

I'LL HAVE A GO NEXT TIME.

THANKS FOR FIXING IT, JIMMY. YOU'RE AN ANGEL.

AW COME ON, LEAVE IT OUT.

SEE YOU DOWN AT THE BIKE MEET ON SUNDAY.

OKAY.

The following week.

WAS THAT THE NEW DUCATI 900SL?

58

60

61

Continued on page 96

MEMORIES OF MY GUY

She flicked through the pages of her past to find the love she had lost.

IT STILL HASN'T STOPPED.

RAINY SATURDAYS ALWAYS GET ME DOWN. YOU SPEND THE WHOLE WEEK WAITING TO BE FREE, THEN, WHEN THE WEEKEND COMES, WHAT HAPPENS? IT RAINS.

MY GUY HASN'T COME EITHER, I'VE GOT NOTHING TO READ — I SUPPOSE I OUGHT TO CLEAN MY ROOM OUT, IT'S BEEN LONG ENOUGH.

THERE ARE A LOT OF COPIES HERE, STILL I'VE HAD *MY GUY* SINCE IT STARTED, THERE OUGHT TO BE.

1978, IT SEEMS SO LONG AGO, I WAS GOING OUT WITH ROGER THEN, I CAN REMEMBER HE ALWAYS WANTED TO BE JOHN TRAVOLTA...HE NEVER QUITE MADE IT.

WHY CAN'T WE PRACTISE IN A PROPER DANCE STUDIO WITH MIRRORS?

BECAUSE I KNOW THE LADY WHO LOOKS AFTER THIS PLACE, DON'T I? A DANCE STUDIO COSTS MONEY.

HAVE YOU GOT THE CASSETTE PLAYER AND THE TAVARES TAPE?

YES, I HAVE GOT THE CASSETTE PLAYER AND THE TAVARES TAPE — WHAT DID YOU THINK I WAS GOING TO DO, HUM IT WHILE WE DANCED?

WHAT DO YOU THINK OF THE SUIT?I GOT IT AT BURTONS, A BIT OF CLASS EH?

HMMM, IT LOOKS VERY EXPENSIVE.

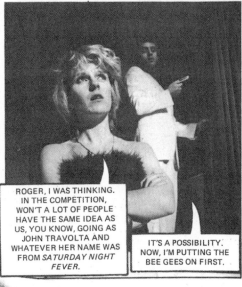

ROGER, I WAS THINKING. IN THE COMPETITION, WON'T A LOT OF PEOPLE HAVE THE SAME IDEA AS US, YOU KNOW, GOING AS JOHN TRAVOLTA AND WHATEVER HER NAME WAS FROM *SATURDAY NIGHT FEVER.*

IT'S A POSSIBILITY. NOW, I'M PUTTING THE BEE GEES ON FIRST.

...SO AFTER WE'VE DONE THAT I MOVE INTO THE SPOTLIGHT ON MY OWN, I GO LIKE THIS AND THE CROWD GO WILD.

HMM, I DON'T BLAME THEM.

IT'S VERY EASY TO DO, YOU JUST ROLL ROUND ME. BUT MIND MY TROUSERS!

OOOOH NO!

I'M LOSING MY BALANCE,

Natalie hadn't seen her friend Jasmine for almost three weeks. And Jasmine had some hot news.

YOU ARE JUST GOING TO DIE WHEN YOU HEAR THIS.

GO ON, YOU'VE BEEN BURSTING TO TELL ME.

WELL, YOU KNOW HOW BIG A FAN I AM OF TOM CRUISE.

I KNOW YOUR ROOM'S PLASTERED WITH POSTERS.

AND I SAW *THE FIRM* FOUR TIMES.

I'VE MET A BOY WITH TOM CRUISE'S EYES - SORT OF.

WHAT WAS HE DOING WITH THEM?

AND HIS EYEBROWS.

"I was just walking through the town centre and they hit me. **Pow!** Like that, right between the eyes."

"And I thought: 'I have **got** to get talking to you'. So I did something really corny. I acted all faint."

THE BOY WITH TOM CRUISE'S EYES — SORT OF

But they weren't the only thing that Jasmine liked about him...

"It was the only thing I could think of."

HEY, ARE YOU OKAY NOW? YOU WERE WOBBLING A BIT THEN.

I-I THINK SO.

ARE YOU CATCHING A BUS OR SOMETHING? I'LL WALK WITH YOU TO THE STOP.

THAT'S VERY KIND OF YOU.

The Photographer's Assistant

Liam had to make a *big* impression...

75

78

WHEELS ON FIRE

Steve took Amanda for a ride
—in more ways than one!

KFH 466

80

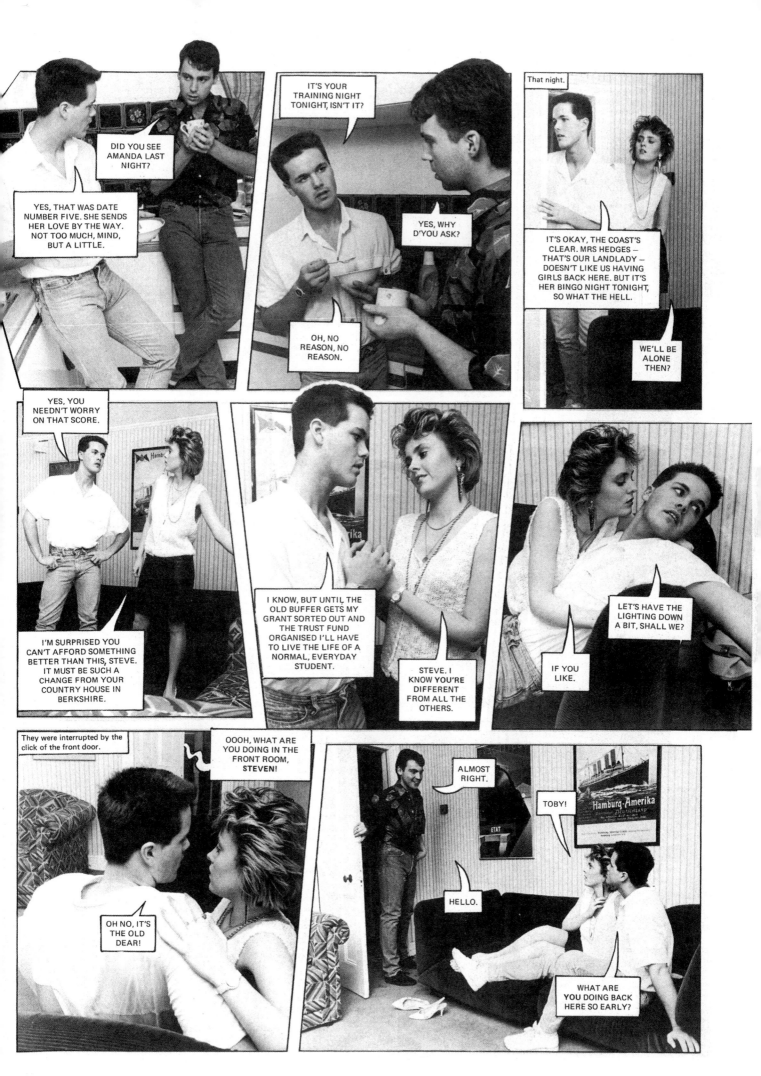

THE GYM GOT DOUBLE BOOKED WITH LADIES HOCKEY SO WE HAD TO CANCEL. WHAT ARE YOU DOING, THOUGH? IT LOOKS FAR MORE INTERESTING.

WHAT DOES IT LOOK LIKE?

I'D LOVE A COFFEE, STEVE.

WHITE NO SUGAR FOR ME, STEVE. WHILE YOU'RE ON YOUR FEET. BISCUITS WOULD BE NICE TOO.

While Steve was out in the kitchen Amanda gossipped about him.

...DIDN'T HE TELL YOU ABOUT THE TROUBLE WITH HIS TRUST FUND? HOW HIS FATHER, THE 7TH BARONET, WON'T RELEASE THE MONEY.

NO, HE DIDN'T. THIS IS ALL NEWS TO ME.

WHAT'S HE BEEN TELLING HER?

IT GOT SO BAD HE ALMOST HAD TO SELL HIS SPORTS CAR. IMAGINE THAT.

HE MUST HAVE IMAGINED THAT, HE CAN'T EVEN DRIVE.

STILL, HE'S SURVIVING.

AMANDA WAS JUST TELLING ME ABOUT THE SPORTS CAR, STEVE. YOU WERE RIGHT NOT TO SELL IT, FERRARIS ARE GOING UP IN VALUE AT THE MOMENT.

ER...YES, I SUPPOSE THEY ARE.

I'D LOVE TO HAVE TO GO IN IT.

SO WOULD I. TAKE US OUT ON SUNDAY.

IT'S NOT DOWN HERE. I LEFT IT AT HOME, THEY'RE RE-TUNING THE ENGINE... THE TURBO'S FAULTY.

NO, IT'S NOT. HE'S JUST BEING MODEST, AMANDA. HE DOESN'T LIKE TAKING IT OUT 'COS IT'S SUCH A CROWD-PULLER. IT'S ROUND THE CORNER.

YOU MUST TAKE ME OUT, STEVE, I INSIST!

CAN I TALK TO YOU IN THE KITCHEN, TOBY?

SURE.

WHAT ARE YOU TRYING TO DO TO ME?

I WAS JUST TRYING TO HELP. YOU'VE OBVIOUSLY MADE UP THIS FANTASTIC STORY ABOUT OWNING A SPORTS CAR. I THOUGHT I'D BACK YOU UP.

I HAVEN'T GOT A SPORTS CAR. YOU KNOW I HAVEN'T GOT A SPORTS CAR. BUT NOW AMANDA THINKS I'VE GOT A SPORTS CAR. WHAT AM I GOING TO DO? YOU'VE GOT TO HELP ME OUT.

BORROW ALAN KENNEDY'S. HE'LL LEND YOU HIS DUTTON. IT'S NOT A FERRARI BUT IT LOOKS FAST.

SHE DOESN'T WANT TO JUST SIT IN IT, THOUGH. SHE WANTS TO GO SOMEWHERE. AND I CAN'T DRIVE.

NO SWEAT. INVITE HER ROUND AND SHOW HER THE CAR, RIGHT? THEN, JUST AS YOU'RE ABOUT TO GO I'LL RUSH OUT AND SAY THE GARAGE IS ON THE PHONE.

86

MURDER BY NUMBERS
Only one girl stood between Alison and the killer!

WHAT'S THE MATTER, WHY THE URGENT PHONE CALL?

I THINK YOU'D BETTER SIT DOWN – IT'S NOT GOOD NEWS.

I'VE JUST HAD A REPORT THAT MADELINE GRAY WAS FOUND DEAD IN A SAUNA. THERE'S A PATTERN BEGINNING TO ESTABLISH ITSELF.

SOMEONE'S PLAYING A MACABRE PRACTICAL JOKE, THEY'RE KILLING THE GIRLS IN REVERSE ORDER, JUST LIKE THE WAY THEY ANNOUNCED THE WINNERS IN THE CONTEST!

SHE WAS THIRD IN THE COMPETITION, THE LAST GIRL TO DIE WAS FOURTH AND THE FIRST GIRL WAS FIFTH.

WHAT DO YOU MEAN?

I DON'T BELIEVE IT... BUT IF IT'S TRUE THAT MEANS THAT JUNE WILL BE NEXT.

WE'RE TRYING TO FIND HER AT THE MOMENT. SINCE I SPOKE TO YOU WE'VE BEEN DOING RESEARCH ON THE COMPETITION. AS SOON AS WE FIND EVERYBODY I'LL BE A LOT HAPPIER.

WHAT'S PUZZLING US AT THE MOMENT IS THE WAY IN WHICH THEY'RE BEING KILLED, EACH ONE'S BEEN COMPLETELY DIFFERENT FROM THE NEXT. WHOEVER'S DOING IT MUST BE PRETTY DERANGED.

SO FOR THE MOMENT I DON'T WANT YOU TO TAKE ANY UNNECESSARY RISKS. DO YOU HAVE TO GO OUT AT ALL?

A FRIEND ASKED ME TO LOOK AFTER HER CAT, SHE ONLY LIVES UP THE ROAD, BUT THERE'S NO-ONE ELSE WHO CAN DO IT.

THAT SHOULD BE ALL RIGHT. AS LONG AS JUNE'S ALIVE, YOU'RE SAFE BUT WE'RE HAVING TROUBLE TRYING TO FIND HER. IF YOU DO SEE ANYTHING SUSPICIOUS THOUGH, GIVE US A RING.

YES OF COURSE.

I WANT TO SEE YOU SAFE AT THE END OF THIS ENQUIRY.

I'M GOING TO SEE THE RUN-THROUGH OF THE BEAUTY COMPETITION FILM. IF ANYTHING COMES IN ON THE GIRL WE'RE LOOKING FOR, I WANT TO KNOW RIGHT AWAY.

AND IN FIRST PLACE, ALISON WILLIAMS FROM CARDIFF!

THERE'S BEEN NOTHING SO FAR – THEY ALL LOOK SWEET AND INNOCENT.

...BUT THOSE TWO DON'T, THEY MUST BE THE FINALISTS WHO WEREN'T PLACED.

He was right, and from the look on their faces they weren't very pleased with the result.

George ran the film through again.

IF YOU'RE A BODY BUILDER YOU COULD ALWAYS COME ROUND AND HELP BUILD MINE.

I WOULDN'T KNOW WHERE TO START.

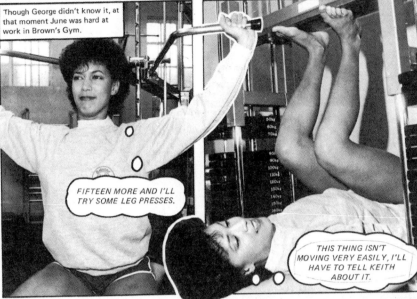

Though George didn't know it, at that moment June was hard at work in Brown's Gym.

FIFTEEN MORE AND I'LL TRY SOME LEG PRESSES.

THIS THING ISN'T MOVING VERY EASILY, I'LL HAVE TO TELL KEITH ABOUT IT.

THAT'S A POINT, WHERE IS KEITH? HE'S NORMALLY HERE TO KEEP AN EYE ON THINGS. . . OH, HANG ON, THIS IS PROBABLY HIM COMING IN NOW.

At Alison's house.

IT'S ABOUT TIME I WENT AND FED COPPER, SHE'LL BE SCRATCHING AT THE DOOR BY NOW.

IT'S HARD TO BELIEVE THAT ANYBODY SHOULD WANT TO KILL YOU – STILL, AS LONG AS JUNE'S SAFE, I'M SAFE.

But June was already dead!

COPPER! – COPPER!

I'D HAVE THOUGHT SHE'D HAVE BEEN WAITING HERE FOR ME.

But somebody else was waiting . . .

DON'T MOVE A MUSCLE!

Continued on Page 143

89

TRUTH GAMES

It took a party game to show Nick how blind he'd been.

91

93

THE END

FAR FROM HOME

James and Sara were on world tours – but going in different directions...

They'd met up outside St. Paul's cathedral and agreed to visit Rye the following day. But first Sara had to get off the hook from her travelling companion.

Sara was making her excuses.

Y'SEE IT'S A CHANCE OF A LIFETIME, VICKI, I'LL NEVER GET THE OPPORTUNITY TO GO AGAIN.

SO YOU'RE NOT COMING TO THE BRITISH MUSEUM?

AND IT'S GOING TO BE REAL HOT TOMORROW... WELL, FOR ENGLAND.

THANKS.

GO ON, THEN GO. I CAN MANAGE ON MY OWN.

WHY ARE YOU PHONING? WHY COULDN'T IT WAIT TILL YOU GOT BACK.

ER... I'VE GOT TO MAKE ARRANGEMENTS.

IT'S BEST NOT TO TELL HER THERE'S A BOY INVOLVED. SHE'D ONLY GET SARCASTIC.

I'LL GIVE JAMES A CHANCE TO GET BACK TO HIS HOSTEL THEN GIVE HIM A CALL.

But she'd left behind one important item.

And it contained his phone number.

HANG ON, WHERE DID I LEAVE MY FILOFAX...?

BY THE PHONE!

AND IT HAD THE NUMBER OF JAMES' HOSTEL. I CAN'T GET IN TOUCH WITH HIM TO MEET UP TOMORROW.

When she got back it had gone.

DAMN, SOMEONE'S TAKEN IT!

OH NO, THIS IS A DISASTER. ALL MY NUMBERS WERE IN THERE, ALL THE ADDRESSES OF THE PEOPLE I'VE MET, EVERYTHING!

WHY DOES THIS ALWAYS HAPPEN TO ME?

Meanwhile. . .

I THINK I'M PROBABLY LOOKING FORWARD TO SEEING HER MORE THAN RYE.

He thought back to when they met.

WHEN I FIRST LOOKED AT YOU I THOUGHT 'SHE'S SCANDINAVIAN'.

OH, DO ME A FAVOUR! DO I LOOK LIKE I OUGHT TO BE IN ABBA.

IT'S SO GREAT TO GET AWAY FROM MUSEUMS, VICKI'S VERY NICE AND SHE MEANS WELL, BUT SHE COULD BORE THE BACKSIDE OFF A RHINO.

SHE COULD, COULD SHE?

Continued on page 146

Continued on page 146

98

Claire went to the park and fell in love...

Claire was out for a walk.

HEY, CLAIRE, WAIT A MINUTE!

Claire had always liked Lee at school — when they were going to school that was.

WHEN THE WIND BLOWS

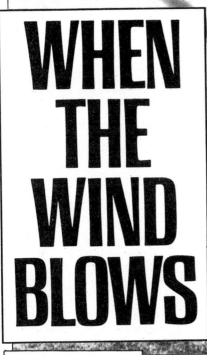

HI, LEE. WHAT ARE YOU DOING IN THIS NECK OF THE WOODS? IT'S THE OTHER SIDE OF TOWN FROM WHERE YOU LIVE, ISN'T IT?

I'VE JUST BEEN ROUND TO MY MATE TONY'S. HE LIVES IN THE NEXT ROAD.

OH, TONY MARCHANT? I KNOW HIM. YOU TWO WERE ALWAYS VERY MATEY AT SCHOOL.

YEAH, THAT'S HIM. ANYWAY, WHERE ARE YOU OFF TO ON A COLD WINTER'S DAY?

I'M GOING TO EAST DEAN PARK. I GO THERE TO GET AWAY FROM MY LITTLE SISTER'S SHAKIN' STEVENS RECORDS — SHE'S GOT THIS PHASE OF PLAYING THEM REALLY LOUD. DO YOU GO UP THERE MUCH?

NO, I'VE NEVER BEEN OUT THIS WAY. I WOULDN'T MIND HAVING A LOOK AT IT, THOUGH. . .

It was hard for Claire to look casual.

MIND. . .? NO, OF COURSE NOT.

IN FACT, IT'S A VERY NICE SURPRISE.

In the park.

I WONDER IF HE REALISED HOW MUCH I FANCIED HIM IN THE FIFTH YEAR?

HEY, THIS IS ALRIGHT. YOU KNOW, IT'S CRAZY, ALL THE YEARS I'VE LIVED IN THE TOWN AND I'VE NEVER EVER BEEN TO THIS PARK.

HARDLY ANYBODY COMES HERE, THAT'S WHY I LIKE IT.

IT'S GOT SOME BEAUTIFUL TREES, LIKE THIS ONE FOR INSTANCE.

IF YOU SAY SO, THEY'RE JUST TREES TO ME.

HOW BIG DO YOU THINK IT IS ROUND THE TRUNK?

I DON'T KNOW. LET'S FIND OUT, SHALL WE? YOU TRY AND PUT YOUR ARMS ROUND FROM THIS SIDE AND I'LL TRY FROM THE OTHER.

OH NO, I'M GOING TO GET DARK STAINS ALL ON MY JUMPER!

YOU'RE SUPPOSED TO BE THE ONE WHO LIKES TREES.

I DON'T THINK WE'RE GOING TO MAKE IT SOMEHOW.

Claire was very slow to let go.

OH, SORRY, I DIDN'T MEAN TO CLING ON.

THAT'S ALRIGHT.

For a second or two, neither of them said a word.

To an outsider it was pretty obvious what they felt for each other, but neither of them wanted to be the first to admit it.

I SUPPOSE I OUGHT TO BE GETTING BACK.

ER, YEAH, ME TOO.

100

But Claire wasn't cross at all.

HE RANG ME. HE ACTUALLY RANG ME!

At the park.

I OUGHT TO THUMP YOU FOR WHAT YOU DID!

OOH, PLEASE — TREAT ME ROUGH.

IN FACT, IT'S SO GOOD I CAN'T THINK OF AN ANSWER. WHY DID **YOU** AGREE TO COME?

NO, I'LL THINK OF SOME OTHER WAY TO GET MY OWN BACK, I'M SURE THERE'S SOME DODGY NICKNAME YOU HAD AT SCHOOL.

LET'S START WALKING SHALL WE?

Claire decided to bring her thoughts into the open.

SO, WHY DID YOU WANT TO SEE ME? WE KNOW IT'S NOT TO DECIDE WHERE THEY'RE GOING TO STICK A BENCH.

HMM, THAT'S A VERY GOOD QUESTION. . .

WELL, YOU MAKE A CHANGE FROM ASTHMATIC OLD MEN AND SWEATY JOGGERS.

THAT'S NICE.

UH OH, I THINK IT'S GOING TO RAIN. I KNEW I SHOULD HAVE BROUGHT A JACKET.

It started to spit with rain and they ran for cover.

QUICK, UNDER HERE!

THERE'S STILL WATER DRIPPING THROUGH. YOU BETTER COME CLOSER.

YOU KNOW, I STILL THINK YOU COULD COME A LITTLE BIT CLOSER.

Claire knew exactly what Lee meant.

I'VE BEEN WANTING HIM TO DO THAT FOR YEARS.

The rain lasted an hour. Claire wished it would last two. Because now she knew. At last they'd shown what they felt for each other.

D'YOU KNOW WHAT, I RECKON THIS IS THE SAME TREE WE CAME TO LAST TIME WE WERE HERE.

IT'S GOT A LOT TO ANSWER FOR THEN.

SHALL I CARVE OUR INITIALS ON IT? HOW DOES IT GO 'CLAIRE FOR LEE...'

NO, DON'T YOU DARE!

YOU MUSTN'T HARM IT.

I DON'T WANT ANYTHING TO HAPPEN TO IT – THIS IS THE PLACE WHERE I FELL IN LOVE.

That had been back in the summer. For weeks afterwards they were inseparable.

D'YOU FANCY GOING FOR A ROW ON THE RIVER.

NO, I DON'T. LAST TIME WE GOT THE LEAKY BOAT AND IT ALMOST RUINED A PAIR OF SHOES. LET'S STICK TO THE RIVER BANK.

Lee was always messing about.

WHAT DO YOU CALL A DEER WITH NO EYES?

I GIVE IN.

NO IDEA. – D'YOU GEDDIT? NO EYE DEAR.

It seemed to Claire that she spent half the summer in East Dean Park.

Walking and walking with Lee.

But then came the stupid argument. Claire had arranged a foursome with her friend Lucy.

WHAT DO YOU MEAN YOU CAN'T MAKE IT! I'VE SET IT ALL UP. PAUL'S TAKEN AN EVENING OFF WORK. I'LL LOOK REALLY STUPID IF I SAY IT'S ALL OFF.

103

104

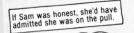

LIFE'S a Beach...

On an empty beach, Sam couldn't afford to be fussy. But then she saw him

109

The 12 Gol Photo

Behind every succesful media format, there are a set of golden rules. Aspiring writers and photographers can learn much from these photo-story basics ...

1. Balancing on one foot looks more realistic than actually running.

2. Wigs add to the realism of a scene.

3. Giving someone a hat immediately makes them Amer

4. Mothers can be any age.

5. Nineteenth century pugilism goes down well in action sequences.

6. Scary tee

. . .and relaxing

. . .and just enjoying being on her own.

As they were about to go. . .

I'M NOT COMING TO THE PARTY, I'M GOING BACK TO THE GRAVEYARD, ON MY OWN!

8. Any kind of headgear will fit in a VW Beetle.

9. Whatever you do – don't change the story to fit the weather.

WHAT ARE YOU LOOKING AT? HAVEN'T YOU SEEN A GORILLA ON A BUS BEFORE?

THERE'S NOTHING LIKE A GOOD BURN-UP!

YOU!

SOMETIMES I THINK YOU'RE CRAZY. . .

10. Don't make biker dialogue too believable.

11. Never allow anyone to under act.

7. Old people love a gorilla on a bus.

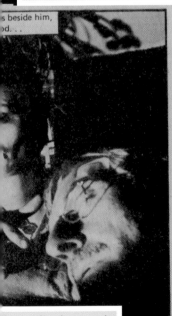

...s beside him, ...d. . .

Then he felt her sharp teet[h] piercing deep into his neck

AAAAAAAAAH!

...ke readers hysterical.

. . .no-one could save him now!

MY GUY COMPLETE PHOTO STORY

A PRACTICAL JOKE BECAME REALITY!

RED ROSE OF DEATH!

He was watching- waiting for his new victim!

12. Romance and bloodshed is always a winner.

111

Our Little Secret

He was everything she was looking for – except for one thing

114

115

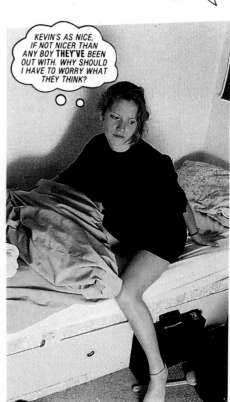

117

Borne On The Wind

Alone in the country, Rebecca had no one to turn to-her destiny was in the hands of others

Rebecca was alone now.

Now her father was buried alongside, in the grave that she had tended since she was a child.

An only child, her mother had died at childbirth.

The years had taught her how to hide her sorrow.

But deep inside, the sadness remained.

And in a world that had never shown her happiness, sadness was no stranger.

WELL NOW, WHO HAVE WE HERE? YOU'RE A PRETTY PICTURE AND NO MISTAKE. WHERE ARE YOU GOING?

I'M GOING TO BIDBURY, SIR.

BIDBURY IS IT? I'M GOING THERE TOO, STEP UP, I'LL TAKE YOU.

NO THANK YOU SIR, I WON'T.

WHAT'S THE MATTER? IT'S A PERFECTLY REASON-ABLE OFFER? YOU'RE NOT AFRAID OF HORSES ARE YOU? COME ON, STEP UP.

I'D LIKE TO BE ALONE.

HAVE IT YOUR OWN WAY, THERE'S MANY A GLOUCESTER GIRL WHO WOULDN'T SAY NO.

Further down the road...

YOU STUPID, LAZY SLUT. CAN'T YOU DO ANYTHING I TELL YOU!

PLEASE SIR, DON'T BEAT ME!

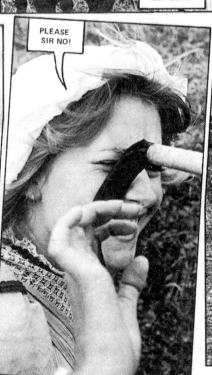

PLEASE SIR NO!

AND IF YOU SO MUCH AS STRAY FROM THE HOUSE AGAIN, YOU'LL KNOW WHAT'S COMING TO YOU!

YES SIR. I WON'T FOR-GET.

119

ARE YOU ALL RIGHT?

YES, LEAVE ME, PLEASE LEAVE ME. I SHALL BE FINE.

At Rebecca's cottage

I DON'T OFTEN GET LETTERS, I WONDER WHAT THIS CAN BE ABOUT?

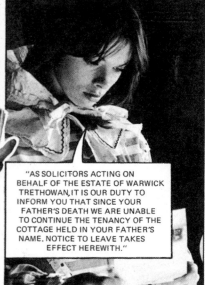

"AS SOLICITORS ACTING ON BEHALF OF THE ESTATE OF WARWICK TRETHOWAN, IT IS OUR DUTY TO INFORM YOU THAT SINCE YOUR FATHER'S DEATH WE ARE UNABLE TO CONTINUE THE TENANCY OF THE COTTAGE HELD IN YOUR FATHER'S NAME. NOTICE TO LEAVE TAKES EFFECT HEREWITH."

HAVE THEY NO PITY? MY FATHER HAS BEEN DEAD THREE WEEKS AND ALREADY THEY ARE ASKING ME TO LEAVE.

I MUST SPEAK TO THIS MR. TRETHOWAN PERSONALLY. I'M SURE HE MUST BE AN UNDERSTANDING MAN.

HE MUST BE WONDERFULLY RICH TO OWN A HOUSE THIS SIZE.

MR. TRETHOWAN?

WELL, LOOK WHO IT IS – MY LITTLE COUNTRY MAID. NOW THIS IS INTERESTING.

MR. TRETHOWAN. . .I. . .I'VE COME TO SEE YOU. . .ABOUT MY FATHER'S COTTAGE.

SO IT'S YOUR COTTAGE IS IT? I WONDERED WHO WE WERE THROWING OUT.

I WONDERED IF I COULD STAY ON THERE – I'M NOT VERY RICH, BUT I WILL PROMISE TO PAY ANYTHING I OWE.

OH NO, YOU CAN'T STAY ON IN THE COTTAGE, THAT'S OUT OF THE QUESTION. BUT IF YOU'VE REALLY GOT NO-WHERE TO LIVE, YOU CAN COME AND LIVE WITH ME!

MY GUY

NOW READ THE SECOND EXCITING CHAPTER!

SHE RAN OUT ON TRETHOWAN—BUT HE KNEW SHE'D BE BACK!

Borne On The Wind

Borne On The Wind was originally published in My Guy four years ago as a serial. It ran over five weeks. However, because the long stories in My Guy Monthly have proved so popular we've run all five episodes together so you can have a second long story this month!

SO YOU WON'T LET ME STAY ON?

WHY SHOULD I? I OWE YOU NO FAVOURS — UNLESS OF COURSE YOU'D LIKE TO FAVOUR ME, THEN WE MIGHT COME TO AN ARRANGEMENT.

For the first time in her sad life Rebecca found love and happiness

WHAT WOULD THAT BE?

YOU REALLY HAVE NO IDEA WHAT I'M TALKING ABOUT, HAVE YOU? SUCH A BEAUTIFUL LITTLE COUNTRY GIRL, SUCH PURITY.

STILL, NOTHING EVER LASTS LONG DOES IT?

LET ME GO!

Rebecca ran from the room close to tears.

YOU CAN'T RUN AWAY FROM ME REBECCA — YOU'VE NOWHERE TO RUN, YOU'LL BE BACK!

But **nothing** would bring Rebecca back to that place.

Borne on the wind of change, Rebecca left home with her few possessions, her destiny was in the hands of others.

Fortune smiled on her, she found work with a farmer in Chilminster. She was miles from home, but at least she was happy.

HELLO, I'M DANIEL, ARE YOU THE NEW GIRL?

YES, I AM.

HOW ARE YOU GETTING ON? I HOPE THE HERD AREN'T GIVING YOU TOO MUCH TROUBLE.

NO, I LIKE WORKING WITH ANIMALS.

YOUR FATHER HAS BEEN VERY KIND TO ME, DANIEL, TAKING ME ON AT SUCH SHORT NOTICE. I'LL NEVER FORGET HIS KINDNESS.

THERE'S NO THANKS NEEDED, WE WANTED SOMEONE, YOU CAME, THAT'S ALL THERE IS TO IT.

I HOPE I CAN STAY HERE, ON THE FARM. ALL MY LIFE I'VE LOOKED FOR HAPPINESS, PERHAPS NOW I'VE FOUND IT.

The weeks flew past on the farm and Daniel and Rebecca were inseparable.

DON'T YOU DROP THOSE NOW.

I WON'T.

Daniel watched Rebecca with love in his eyes.

FORCED TO WORK FOR A MAN SHE HATED!

She had to leave the only love she had ever known for a man she despised!

Borne On The Wind

When this story first appeared as a serial, it would have taken you a nailbiting fortnight to get this far. Luckily now you don't have to wait — you can read it all in one go.

YOU CAN'T JUST TAKE HER!

OH YES I CAN, AND WHAT'S MORE I HAVE AN ORDER TO PROVE IT, YOU'LL FIND IT'S ALL LEGAL.

NOW MOVE ASIDE OR I'LL GET A CONSTABLE TO TAKE HER!

Her bag packed, it was hard for Rebecca to say goodbye.

DON'T CRY, IT'S NOT THE END OF THE WORLD REBECCA. WE'LL STILL BE ABLE TO SEE EACH OTHER.

MY FATHER WON'T LET TRETHOWAN GET AWAY WITH IT JUST LIKE THAT — WILL YOU WRITE TO ME?

OF COURSE I WILL DANIEL, OF COURSE I'LL WRITE. IT'LL BE MY ONLY PLEASURE.

GOODBYE REBECCA, MAY GOD WATCH OVER YOU. TAKE THIS AND REMEMBER ME,

Rebecca's new life was hard.

Trethowan was a hard master and she was to get little rest in the first few weeks.

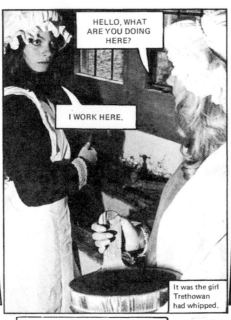

HELLO, WHAT ARE YOU DOING HERE?

I WORK HERE.

It was the girl Trethowan had whipped.

YOU MUST BE MAD, WHAT MADE YOU COME AND WORK FOR HIM!

I HAD TO, I OWE HIM MONEY.

OH, I SEE.

THAT'S HIM CALLING NOW, GO ON, I'LL DO THAT. HE'LL BE WANTING THE POST OR SOMETHING.

HELLO REBECCA, MY WORD I DO LIKE THE UNIFORM, I CAN SEE YOU'RE GOING TO BE A PRETTY ADDITION TO MY STAFF.

WHAT DO YOU WANT SIR?

IF YOU WANT NOTHING I'LL GO BACK TO THE KITCHEN.

DON'T GET FLIGHTY WITH ME. COME BACK HERE!

I CAN SEE YOU HAVEN'T GOT ENOUGH TO DO. CHANGE THE LOGS ON THE FIRE, WHEN YOU'VE FINISHED THAT MAKE THE BEDS AND AFTERWARDS THERE ARE SHEETS THAT WANT LAUNDERING. I CAN SEE YOU WANT A LESSON IN MANNERS TOO.

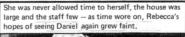

She was never allowed time to herself, the house was large and the staff few — as time wore on, Rebecca's hopes of seeing Daniel again grew faint.

"PRAY FOR ME DANIEL. TRETHOWAN MAKES ME WORK ALL HOURS OF THE DAY. SOMETIMES I FEEL VERY WEAK FROM IT, BUT KNOWING THAT YOU ARE READING THIS MAKES ME STRONG. HE DOES NOT LET ME OUT AND RECENTLY HE HAS MADE ADVANCES. DANIEL, WRITE TO ME AND TELL ME THAT YOU CARE."

WHY DON'T YOU MARRY ME. IT CAN'T BE WORSE THAN WHAT YOU'RE GOING THROUGH NOW. IF YOU MARRY ME, YOU DON'T HAVE TO BE MY SERVANT ANY MORE, YOU COULD BE A FREE WOMAN. WELL, WHAT DO YOU SAY?

I HAVE NOTHING TO SAY TO YOU.

SHE'LL COME ROUND TO IT, JUST GIVE IT TIME. SHE'S ONLY HAD SIX MONTHS OF HELL, SHE WON'T BE SO ANXIOUS TO SAY NO IN ANOTHER SIX MONTHS TIME.

The months passed by and still Rebecca had no news of Daniel.

"DANIEL WHY DON'T YOU WRITE TO ME? IT'S BEEN EIGHT MONTHS NOW. DO YOU REALLY CARE WHAT HAPPENS TO ME? I WAIT FOR DAYS AND DAYS AND STILL NO ANSWER COMES. I LOVE YOU DEARLY, BUT I CANNOT BEAR YOUR SILENCE.

MARRY ME REBECCA, SURELY IT'S BETTER THAN YOUR PRESENT EXISTENCE.

IT'S NO USE THINKING ABOUT YOUR FARM BOY. HE DOESN'T LOVE YOU. IF HE DID, HE WOULD HAVE WRITTEN. MARRY ME, REBECCA, MARRY ME TOMORROW.

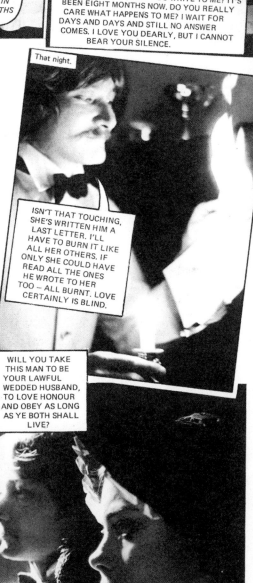

That night.

ISN'T THAT TOUCHING, SHE'S WRITTEN HIM A LAST LETTER. I'LL HAVE TO BURN IT LIKE ALL HER OTHERS. IF ONLY SHE COULD HAVE READ ALL THE ONES HE WROTE TO HER TOO — ALL BURNT. LOVE CERTAINLY IS BLIND.

WILL YOU TAKE THIS MAN TO BE YOUR LAWFUL WEDDED HUSBAND, TO LOVE HONOUR AND OBEY AS LONG AS YE BOTH SHALL LIVE?

Next day, in church.

YOU STAND HERE IN THE SIGHT OF GOD...

Outside.

THE GIRL AT THE HOUSE SAID SHE'D BE AT THE CHURCH THIS MORNING, I WONDER WHAT SHE'S DOING IN THERE? IT SOUNDS AS THOUGH THERE'S A SERVICE GOING ON.

MY GUY

NOW READ THE FOURTH EXCITING CHAPTER!

TRAPPED BY A MAN SHE COULD NEVER LOVE!

Love arrived too late for Rebecca —she has bound herself to another!

Borne On The Wind

Borne On The Wind was originally published in My Guy as a serial, running over five weeks. Now we've put all five episodes together to make one extra long story.

... SO LONG AS YE BOTH SHALL LIVE, SO HELP ME GOD?

I WILL.

WELL, HOW DOES IT FEEL TO BE MRS. TRETHOWAN?

IT FEELS NOTHING AT ALL. YOU HAVE MY NAME, MY SOUL YOU WILL NEVER HAVE.

YOU'VE SWORN TO LOVE, HONOUR AND OBEY ME AND I'LL HAVE YOUR LOVE, HONOUR AND OBEDIENCE!

But as they made their way from the church.

DANIEL!

WHAT HAVE YOU DONE?

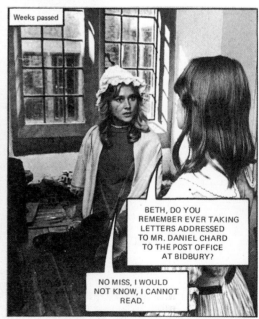

IS THAT THE MAN YOU LOVED WHEN YOU FIRST CAME HERE, THE MAN YOU USED TO CRY ABOUT, NIGHT AFTER NIGHT?

YES, I USED TO WRITE HIM LONG LETTERS, TELLING HIM MY WILDEST DREAMS. WHEN YOU'VE NOTHING BUT HOPE TO LIVE ON, DREAMS ARE BRIGHT STARS IN THE SKY AND HOPE GIVES YOU THE COURAGE TO BELIEVE THAT SOME DAY THEY'LL COME TRUE.

NOW I THINK OF IT, I NEVER TOOK LETTERS OTHER THAN IN THE MASTER'S HANDWRITING, AND I CAN REMEMBER MRS. BUNTING SAYING YOU HAD A LETTER ONCE, I THOUGHT IT ODD, BECAUSE SERVANTS AREN'T SUPPOSED TO GET LETTERS.

SO HE DID DESTROY THEM! HE TRULY IS AN EVIL MAN.

YOU OUGHT TO LEAVE MISS. I WOULD IF I WERE YOU. I HATE HIM, HE GAVE ME THIS TO REMIND ME HOW MUCH. LEAVE MISS, BEFORE HE GETS TIRED OF YOU AND TREATS YOU THE WAY HE TREATS ME.

That night, Rebecca found the flower Danial had given her.

DUST, IT'S NOTHING BUT DUST. I MUST LEAVE HERE AND SEE HIM, OR MY LIFE WILL BE DUST LIKE THIS FLOWER. I CANNOT LIVE A DAY LONGER WITHOUT SEEING DANIEL.

So, packing a bag, she left.

She walked through the night, and next morning reached Daniel's farm.

IT'S REBECCA ISN'T IT? WE HAVEN'T SEEN YOU IN A LONG WHILE.

MRS CHARD, I'VE COME TO SEE DANIEL.

I'M AFRAID YOU CAN'T DO THAT, HE'S SET OFF FOR BRISTOL. HE'S MADE UP HIS MIND THIS COUNTRY'S NOT FOR HIM. HE'S GOING TO CANADA.

WHEN DID HE GO?

HE LEFT TWO DAYS AGO.

DANIEL... WILL I EVER SEE YOU AGAIN?

Advertisement

Get rid of warts painlessly, without cutting or cauterization. Compound W* is a clear colourless liquid which penetrates into the common wart, removing it painlessly. Your skin will quickly be soft and smooth again. Compound W from all chemists.

Compound W 🅦

* Trade Mark.

Advertisement

Is every month going to be as difficult?

You're well on the way to being a woman. Having periods really is the proof of that. But no one told you that periods can be painful. And when they are they make you miserable and irritable. It's then that you might feel that boys have the better deal. But many women just won't put up with it. They might not tell you, but they take something to help them over those bad days. They take 'Anadin'* Tablets, the all-round pain reliever. Its modern, balanced formula is based on a combination of laboratory-tested ingredients. 'Anadin' relieves pain and so relaxes tension and leaves you feeling yourself again. That's why the 'Anadin' formula is especially suitable for period pains.

Next time you go to the chemist's, get some 'Anadin' Tablets. You'll find, like so many women, that 'Anadin' can help make one day of the month seem just like any other.

Trade mark

MY GUY CHAPTER FIVE — DANIEL WAS BOUND

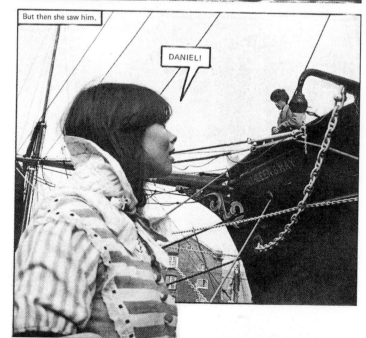

130

Borne On the Wind

If she couldn't have Daniel, Rebecca didn't want to live at all.

Here it is — the last exciting chapter of the story which would have taken you five weeks to read originally. Now you don't have to wait to find out how it all ends . . .

DANIEL, IT'S ME, REBECCA!

WHAT ARE YOU DOING HERE?

OH DANIEL, I THOUGHT I'D NEVER SEE YOU AGAIN.

WHY HAVE YOU COME?

I HAD TO SEE YOU. ALL THIS TIME WE'VE BEEN APART TRETHOWAN WAS DESTROYING OUR LETTERS. I USED TO WRITE TO YOU AND NEVER GOT A REPLY. YOU WROTE TO ME AND HEARD NOTHING. BUT ALL THE TIME I LOVED YOU.

NOW HOLD ON. YOU MARRIED A MAN YOU HATED, A MAN YOU COULD NEVER LOVE, IF THAT'S NOT A TOKEN OF YOUR REAL VALUE I DON'T KNOW WHAT IS.

HE MADE MY LIFE MISERABLE DANIEL, YOU CAN'T IMAGINE THE PAIN I LIVED THROUGH. WHEN I DIDN'T HEAR FROM YOU HE BEGAN TO TELL ME THAT YOU DIDN'T LOVE ME. I SHOULDN'T HAVE BELIEVED HIM, BUT WHEN MONTHS PASSED AND I STILL HEARD NOTHING AND STILL HE ASKED, IT WAS HARD TO REFUSE HIM. I RAN OUT OF REASONS TO SAY NO.

BUT WHAT CAN BE DONE? IT ALL SEEMS SO HOPELESS. I'M A MARRIED WOMAN AND NO ACCOUNT OF HIS EVIL WILL EVER BREAK THE FACT THAT I'M HIS AND NOT YOURS. PERHAPS WE SHOULD KILL OURSELVES, IT WOULD BE ONE END TO OUR MISERY.

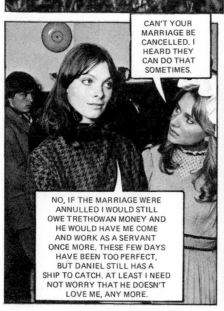

CAN'T YOUR MARRIAGE BE CANCELLED. I HEARD THEY CAN DO THAT SOMETIMES.

NO, IF THE MARRIAGE WERE ANNULLED I WOULD STILL OWE TRETHOWAN MONEY AND HE WOULD HAVE ME COME AND WORK AS A SERVANT ONCE MORE. THESE FEW DAYS HAVE BEEN TOO PERFECT, BUT DANIEL STILL HAS A SHIP TO CATCH. AT LEAST I NEED NOT WORRY THAT HE DOESN'T LOVE ME, ANY MORE.

COME BACK WITH ME DANIEL, SURELY YOU WON'T LEAVE ME NOW, NOW I NEED YOU MORE THAN EVER I DID. I CAN'T TELL YOU EVERYTHING HERE OR DO JUSTICE TO MY STORY IN THE FEW HOURS BEFORE YOU SAIL. YOU MAY NOT LIKE ME FOR WHAT I'VE DONE, BUT STAY IF ONLY TO UNDERSTAND WHY I DID IT.

THERE SHOULD BE A CLIPPER NEXT WEEK. I'LL TAKE THAT. EXPLAIN AWAY.

Later that day.

I HEARD YOU WERE BACK MISS.

HOW DID YOU KNOW THAT?

IT'S ALL ROUND THE VILLAGE, NEWS TRAVELS QUICKER THAN YOU THINK.

There was a sharp tap at the door.

SO REBECCA, WE MEET AGAIN. GOOD DAY TO YOU FARMER, NOW IF YOU DON'T MIND, I'VE COME FOR MY WIFE...

NO!

Rebecca convinced Daniel and together they returned home to the farm.

I HAVE DONE YOU A GREAT WRONG. I CAN SEE THAT NOW. WHEN I THINK OF ALL THE NIGHTS WE COULD HAVE BEEN TOGETHER AND THAT MAN KEPT US APART.

I CANNOT STAND TO SEE YOU SO SAD MISS — DANIEL'S THE MAN YOU LOVE, ISN'T HE? THE ONE THAT USED TO WRITE YOU THE LETTERS.

YES.

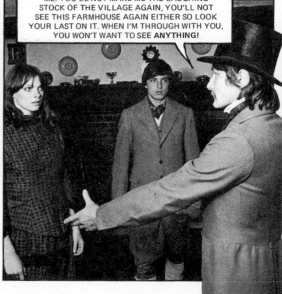

COME ON REBECCA YOU'RE COMING HOME WITH ME. YOU'LL NOT MAKE ME THE LAUGHING STOCK OF THE VILLAGE AGAIN, YOU'LL NOT SEE THIS FARMHOUSE AGAIN EITHER SO LOOK YOUR LAST ON IT. WHEN I'M THROUGH WITH YOU, YOU WON'T WANT TO SEE **ANYTHING!**

TALES OF THE RIVERBANK

Danny and Peter went joyriding - in a cabin cruiser!

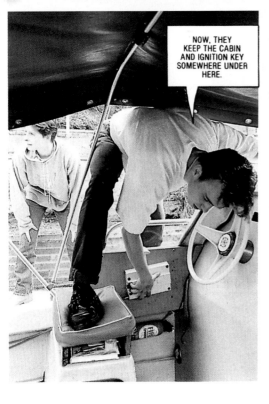

135

137

138

Lynne's diary revealed things that were...

BEST KEPT SECRET

It was breaktime at Althorpe Comprehensive.

Lynne didn't have any special friends.

HERE, KERRY, WHY DO YOU RECKON LYNNE TAYLOR ALWAYS HANGS ROUND HERE AT BREAK?

GOD, I THOUGHT THE BELL WOULD NEVER GO. LET'S DUMP THIS STUFF IN THE FORM ROOM AND GO AND SEE MARK AND TONY.

OKAY, KERRY. WE'LL HAVE TO BE QUICK, THOUGH. IT'S MATHS NEXT.

SEARCH ME, TRACE. IF SHE WON'T MIX WITH THE REST OF US, IT'S HER OWN FAULT SHE'S MISERABLE.

But Lynne wasn't miserable.

NOW EVERYONE'S GONE, I CAN WRITE UP YESTERDAY.

I CAN TELL MY DIARY ANYTHING I WANT. IT'S MUCH BETTER THAN PEOPLE. THEY CALL THEMSELVES FRIENDS, THEN BITCH ABOUT YOU THE MOMENT YOU'RE GONE.

I CAN SAY THINGS I'D NEVER BE ABLE TO TELL A LIVING SOUL TO MY DIARY, THINGS ABOUT IAN. THINGS THAT WON'T BE REPEATED.

She poured out her thoughts about Ian on almost every page.

AND I BET HE HARDLY KNOWS I EXIST. STILL, THERE GOES THE BELL-TIME TO STOP! I CAN FINISH IT OFF LATER.

HERE, WHAT'S THAT YOU'RE WRITING? NOT DOING EXTRA WORK, ARE YOU?

NO, THAT'S NOT A SCHOOLBOOK, THAT'S A DIARY. LET'S HAVE A LOOK THEN!

GET OFF! LEAVE IT ALONE! YOU CAN'T LOOK — IT'S PRIVATE.

OH, YEAH?

WHAT HAVE YOU GOT TO WRITE IN A DIARY? YOU NEVER DO ANYTHING, DO YOU?

YEAH, WHO WANTS TO READ YOUR RUBBISH, ANYWAY? I BET IT WOULD SEND US TO SLEEP.

YEAH, WELL, YOU'LL NEVER KNOW, WILL YOU?

At lunchtime. . .

I WOULDN'T PUT IT PAST THOSE TWO TO NICK MY DIARY OUT OF MY BAG.

IT'LL BE SAFER IN HERE. UNDER LOCK AND KEY!

Lynne didn't see Tracy and Kerry outside.

SHE PUT HER DIARY IN HER LOCKER. QUICK, GIVE US YOUR NAIL FILE, KERRY.

OKAY, TRACE, BUT MAKE IT QUICK — SHE MIGHT COME BACK.

NOW WE'LL FIND OUT WHY SHE HAS TO KEEP IT LOCKED UP. MAYBE IT'S HOT STUFF!

LET'S HAVE A LOOK!

141

THERE'S ONLY THREE PAGES HERE. BUT THERE WERE FOUR MISSING. WHAT HAVE THEY DONE WITH THE OTHER ONE?

LOST SOMETHING, LYNNE?

YEAH, LIKE MARCH FOURTH? THAT WAS A VERY HOT DAY, AS I RECALL. . .

WHAT HAVE YOU DONE WITH IT, YOU COW?

WHAT DO YOU THINK? I'VE SENT IT TO IAN FORDHAM. I THOUGHT HE OUGHT TO KNOW PEOPLE WERE WRITING THINGS ABOUT HIM. HE'LL GET IT TOMORROW!

Lynne had a very sleepless night.

I USED TO LONG TO BUMP INTO IAN. I'LL JUST DIE OF SHAME IF I SEE HIM NOW.

HI, LYNNE.

IT'S HIM! OH, NO — I CAN'T BEAR IT!

It was almost as if he was waiting for her.

HELLO, I'VE BEEN READING WHAT YOU WROTE.

I—I'M SORRY, I FEEL SO EMBARRASSED. ARE YOU VERY ANGRY?

ANGRY? WHY SHOULD I BE? YOU WROTE SOME REALLY NICE THINGS ABOUT ME. WHY DIDN'T YOU EVER LET ON THAT YOU FELT THAT WAY?

I COULDN'T. I'M JUST TOO SHY, YOU SEE. MY DIARY WAS THE ONLY PLACE WHERE I COULD SAY WHAT I FELT.

YOU'LL HAVE TO TELL ME ALL ABOUT IT. WHY DON'T WE MEET HERE AFTER SCHOOL — OKAY?

OKAY. . .I MEAN, YES!

Lynne didn't know what would happen with Ian, but she felt sure of one thing. . .

. . .From now on, her diary wouldn't be her only friend.

MURDER BY NUMBERS

George has minutes to solve the mystery, if he's to save Alison!

George continued to watch the film.

YOU'RE VERY NERVOUS AREN'T YOU?

I CAN'T SEE A THING WITHOUT MY GLASSES, I'D LIKE TO HAVE CONTACT LENSES BUT I'M NOT SUITABLE.

I LOVE TO TAKE A LONG HOT BATH

IF YOU EVER WANT SOMEONE TO SCRUB YOUR BACK, I'LL GIVE YOU MY PHONE NUMBER.

George thought back — Judy was found dead in the bath!

SHE LIKES NOTHING BETTER THAN TO RELAX IN A SAUNA — WELL IT CERTAINLY HASN'T SHRUNK HER!

Madeline was killed in the sauna!

THAT'S FUNNY, I CAN'T REMEMBER SEEING ANYTHING IN THE FORENSIC REPORT ABOUT GLASSES BEING FOUND. THERE WERE CERTAINLY NONE IN THE HOUSE WHEN SHE WAS KILLED.

143

FAR FROM HOME

James had met up with Sara, another Aussie tourist on a world tour. They'd agreed to visit Rye, but Sara lost his phone number. Then, when he thought she'd lost interest, they ran into each other at Rye station.

James and Sara escape the city to explore Rye...

THEN THIS MORNING I SUDDENLY REMEMBERED THE NAME OF YOUR HOSTEL, LOOKED IT UP IN THE BOOK. . . AND HERE I AM.

I'M SORRY I DIDN'T PHONE YOU, I GOT MY FILOFAX STOLEN, I'VE BEEN GOING CRAZY WITHOUT IT.

I PUT IT DOWN FOR TWO MINUTES, CAN YOU BELIEVE IT? TWO MINUTES AND IT WENT.

SO HOW DID YOU KNOW I'D BE HERE?

I RANG YOUR HOSTEL, THEY SAID YOU'D GONE TO RYE.

IT'S A LUCKY BREAK.

OH, SO THAT'S IT.

I WISH I COULD GET ALL MY NUMBERS BACK.

SOME OF THOSE NUMBERS ARE FROM PEOPLE I'VE MET GOING ROUND THE WORLD. I'LL NEVER GET THEM BACK.

147

Continued on page 176

148

The Driving Instructor

Stephanie was trying to keep her eyes on the road but the guy next to her drove her to distraction

Stephanie was having a driving lesson...

HE SHOULD BE HERE ANY MINUTE

WELL I HOPE YOU KNOW WHAT YOU'RE DOING

...but her sister wasn't sure if it was the right thing.

YOU'RE STUPID. WHY DON'T YOU JUST ASK HIM FOR A DATE INSTEAD OF HAVING DRIVING LESSONS

IT'S ALL RIGHT, I'M ONLY HAVING ONE

THERE'S A CAR JUST PULLED UP, IT'S HIM

I HOPE I LOOK ALL RIGHT

149

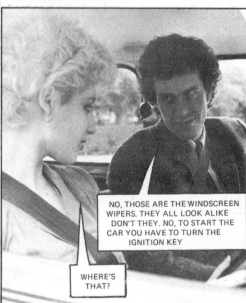

Later that morning.

MR. DAVIS YOU SAID WE WERE GOING TO USE QUIET ROADS, THERE'S A LOT OF TRAFFIC BEHIND ME

DON'T WORRY, THEY'LL GO AWAY

GOD WILLING

WELL NOW, WE'VE FINISHED THREE POINT TURNS. I'D LIKE YOU TO MOVE OFF IN YOUR OWN TIME. REMEMBER THE ROUTINE — MIRROR, SIGNAL, MANOEUVRE

HE'S SO FIRM AND DECISIVE

It was too late.

Stephanie was still daydreaming as the car moved off. . .

YOU FORGOT THE MIRROR!

EASI-DRIVE SCHOOL OF MOTORING

A car flashed past them.

DID HE HIT US?

NO, HE MANAGED TO TAKE AVOIDING ACTION— BUT THE THREE CARS HE DID HIT DON'T LOOK TOO PLEASED

At the end of the lesson.

HE WON'T ASK ME FOR A DATE, SO I'LL HAVE TO ASK HIM

MR. DAVIS WOULD YOU LIKE TO COME—

YES, WHAT IS IT?

. . .COME. . .ER. . .FOR ANOTHER DRIVING LESSON NEXT WEEK?

YES, I'D LOVE TO

DAMN, I'LL HAVE TO WORK UP MORE COURAGE NEXT TIME

. . .and on. . .

WHAT'S THE FIRST THING YOU DO WHEN YOU GET INTO THE CAR?

STRAIGHTEN MY SKIRT?

t the lessons went on. . .

WHAT GEAR ARE YOU IN?

IT'S A SORT OF RED BLOUSE

. . .and on. . .

NO!!!!!

. . .and still Stephanie hadn't asked him for a date.

151

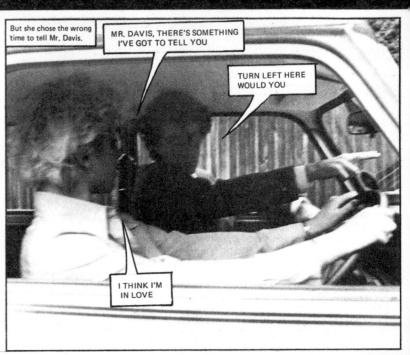

They began to walk home.

YOU KNOW WHEN I TELL THEM IN THE OFFICE ABOUT YOU, NOBODY BELIEVES ME — THEY WON'T BELIEVE THIS

YOU TELL THEM ABOUT ME?

OH YES, I'VE NEVER MET ANYONE QUITE LIKE YOU BEFORE. I ALWAYS WONDER WHAT YOU'RE GOING TO DO NEXT.

WELL HE WON'T HAVE GUESSED THIS ONE

HE HASN'T LEAPT AWAY, THIS MUST BE ONE SURPRISE HE'S ENJOYED!

I'M SORRY, I HAD TO DO THAT. I TRIED TO TELL YOU BEFORE BUT YOU WEREN'T LISTENING

THAT'S ALL RIGHT. BUT PROMISE YOU WON'T FORGET TO DO IT TONIGHT WHEN I TAKE YOU OUT!

At long last, Stephanie had got her date!

SO IT'S 8.30 OUTSIDE MY PLACE

YES, IF THE DRIVING LESSONS HAVE BEEN ANYTHING TO GO BY, IT SHOULD BE QUITE AN EVENING

But one thing stood in their way.

OH NO, I'VE JUST REMEMBERED, I HAVEN'T GOT A CAR NOW, WE'LL HAVE TO CALL IT OFF

IT'S ALL RIGHT, WE CAN USE MINE

BUT YOU CAN'T DRIVE

YES I CAN, I'VE BEEN DRIVING FOR TWO YEARS— STILL THE LESSONS WERE VERY ENJOYABLE, THOUGH I WAS A BIT NERVOUS

SEE — HERE ARE THE KEYS

I DON'T BELIEVE IT

SEE YOU TONIGHT

I JUST DON'T BELIEVE IT!

THE END

153

NEVER TEAR US APART

Emma was determined her parents **wouldn't** interfere with her life...

It wasn't hard to spot that Emma was in love.

ARE YOU GOING TO COME IN?

I'VE GOT TO GET BACK. MY COUSIN'S IN THE ARMY Y'SEE AND IT'S HIS LAST NIGHT ON LEAVE. I SAID I'D SEE HIM OFF.

BUT I PROMISE I'LL COME IN NEXT TIME.

YOU BETTER.

I WILL

Inside.

DO YOU WANT TO TELL ME ABOUT HIM? IT LOOKED FAIRLY SERIOUS FROM WHERE I WAS WATCHING.

YOU'RE SUCH A NOSEY OLD COW, MUM!

154

155

156

157

THE END

DUMMY RUN

Maria needed someone to find out about a boy...

CAN YOU REMEMBER WHICH ONE OF THOSE BOYS WAS CALLED 'ALAN'?

WHAT ARE YOU ON ABOUT?

YOU KNOW, ON SATURDAY, THE BOYS WHO WERE TRYING TO CHAT US UP.

I'VE SLEPT SINCE. WHY D'YOU WANT TO KNOW?

ONE OF THEM RANG ME UP AND ASKED ME OUT.

AND YOU DON'T KNOW WHICH ONE IT WAS. YOU MUST HAVE BEEN FAR GONE.

161

163

IF · LEAVING · ME · IS · EASY

When Alex walked out of her life, Emma wanted one question answered–why?

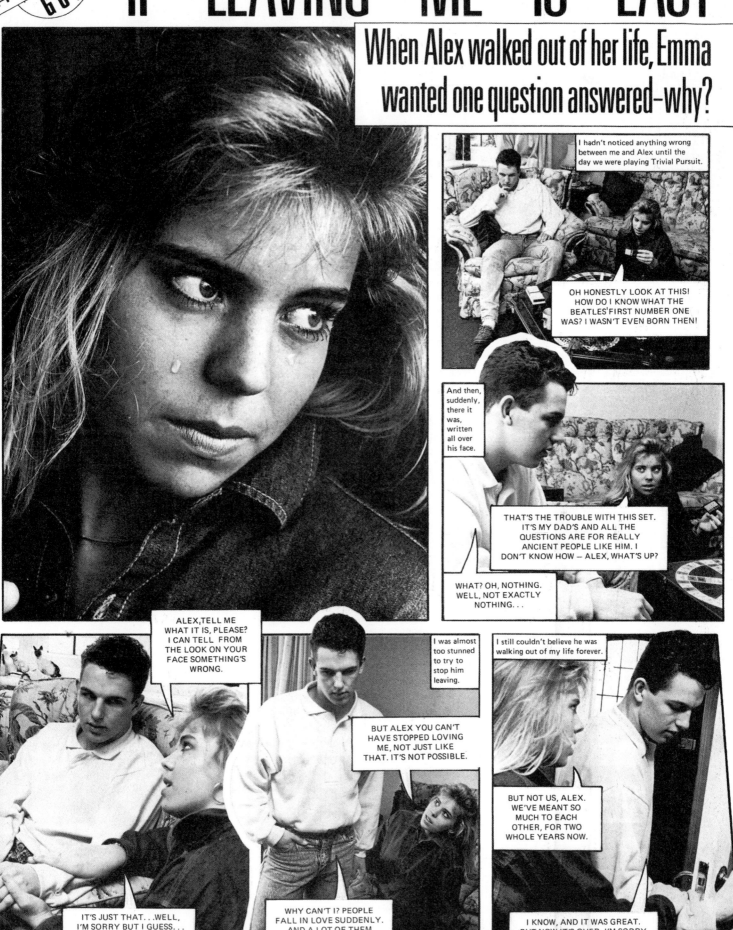

I hadn't noticed anything wrong between me and Alex until the day we were playing Trivial Pursuit.

OH HONESTLY LOOK AT THIS! HOW DO I KNOW WHAT THE BEATLES' FIRST NUMBER ONE WAS? I WASN'T EVEN BORN THEN!

And then, suddenly, there it was, written all over his face.

THAT'S THE TROUBLE WITH THIS SET. IT'S MY DAD'S AND ALL THE QUESTIONS ARE FOR REALLY ANCIENT PEOPLE LIKE HIM. I DON'T KNOW HOW — ALEX, WHAT'S UP?

WHAT? OH, NOTHING. WELL, NOT EXACTLY NOTHING. . .

ALEX, TELL ME WHAT IT IS, PLEASE? I CAN TELL FROM THE LOOK ON YOUR FACE SOMETHING'S WRONG.

IT'S JUST THAT. . .WELL, I'M SORRY BUT I GUESS. . . I GUESS I JUST DON'T LOVE YOU ANY MORE.

I was almost too stunned to try to stop him leaving.

BUT ALEX YOU CAN'T HAVE STOPPED LOVING ME, NOT JUST LIKE THAT. IT'S NOT POSSIBLE.

WHY CAN'T I? PEOPLE FALL IN LOVE SUDDENLY. AND A LOT OF THEM FALL OUT OF LOVE THE SAME WAY.

I still couldn't believe he was walking out of my life forever.

BUT NOT US, ALEX. WE'VE MEANT SO MUCH TO EACH OTHER, FOR TWO WHOLE YEARS NOW.

I KNOW, AND IT WAS GREAT. BUT NOW IT'S OVER. I'M SORRY EMMA, BUT THAT'S JUST THE WAY IT IS.

I knew we'd been happy. That was why what had just happened didn't make any sense.

I'VE GOT TO KNOW WHY, I'VE JUST **GOT** TO. HE OUGHT TO TELL ME. EVEN IF HE'S IN LOVE WITH SOMEONE ELSE NOW. HE OWES ME THAT MUCH AFTER ALL WE'VE BEEN THROUGH.

It took me a whole day to work up the courage to ring him.

IT'S NO GOOD, I'VE GOT TO DO IT. IF HE TELLS ME TO GET LOST, I WON'T BE ANY WORSE OFF.

But it was all for nothing.

OH, HELLO MRS. WILLIAMS, IT'S ME, EMMA. IS. . .ER. . . ALEX IN PLEASE?

NO, HE WENT OUT HALF AN HOUR AGO, I COULDN'T SAY WHERE, THOUGH, HE NEVER TELLS ME ANYTHING. I'LL GET HIM TO RING YOU.

But three days later he still hadn't rung.

I CAN'T BELIEVE HE'S JUST IGNORED ME – BUT HIS MUM'S ALWAYS VERY GOOD ABOUT PASSING ON MESSAGES, SO HE MUST HAVE GOT IT. IT'S NO USE, I'LL HAVE TO TRY AGAIN.

My heart was in my mouth as I dialled. I longed to hear his voice again, but I was terrified of what he might say.

AND IF HE'S NOT THERE I CAN ASK HIS MUM. SHE MUST KNOW WHAT'S GOING ON.

I got his mum.

NO, EMMA, YOU'VE MISSED HIM AGAIN. DIDN'T HE RING YOU AFTER LAST TIME? WELL, I GAVE HIM THE MESSAGE. . .

PERHAPS YOU CAN HELP ME, MRS. WILLIAMS. WE'VE SPLIT UP YOU SEE. DO YOU KNOW WHY? HAS HE SAID ANYTHING?

OH, I AM SORRY EMMA. I DIDN'T KNOW. HE'S SAID NOTHING TO ME. BUT THEN, YOU KNOW OUR ALEX, KEEPS THINGS VERY CLOSE TO HIS CHEST. LIKE HIS FATHER IN THAT RESPECT, NOW ME, I'M JUST THE OPPOSITE. . .

His mother knew less than I did. But someone, somewhere had to know.

PAUL'S HIS BEST MATE. THEY TELL EACH OTHER EVERYTHING. HE'D KNOW IF ALEX HAD ANOTHER GIRL OR ANYTHING. IF I HURRY I CAN CATCH HIM AS HE LEAVES WORK.

Paul was coming out of the hi-fi shop where he worked.

EMMA, WHAT ARE YOU DOING HERE? IF YOU'VE COME TO BUY A WORD PROCESSOR YOU'RE TOO LATE, WE'RE CLOSED. ACTUALLY HALF OF THEM DON'T WORK ANYWAY...

PAUL, LISTEN TO ME, THIS IS SERIOUS. ALEX HAS. . .WELL, ALEX AND I HAVE SPLIT UP. AND I DON'T KNOW WHY.

I'M SORRY EMMA, I DIDN'T KNOW. HE HASN'T MENTIONED IT TO ME.

I JUST DON'T UNDER-STAND PAUL, WHAT'S THE BIG MYSTERY? DON'T YOU HAVE ANY IDEA? IS THERE SOMEONE ELSE? ANOTHER GIRL?

I WON'T BE CROSS EVEN IF THERE IS. I JUST WANT TO KNOW.

WELL, LIKE I SAID I DIDN'T EVEN KNOW ABOUT YOU TWO. HE HASN'T SAID ANYTHING ABOUT ANOTHER GIRL, BUT I RECKON I'D HAVE HEARD IF THERE WAS SOMEONE.

BUT WHY ELSE WOULD HE FINISH WITH ME SO SUDDENLY? IT WASN'T LIKE THINGS HAD BEEN GOING WRONG BETWEEN US OR WE'D HAD A ROW. THINK, PAUL, IS THERE ANYTHING HE'S SAID THAT MIGHT TELL ME?

IT'S NO GOOD, IT'S A TOTAL MYSTERY TO ME TOO. BUT THEN, EVEN THOUGH WE'RE BEST MATES, HE DOESN'T TELL ME EVERYTHING. YOU KNOW ALEX. HE'S GOT THAT SECRETIVE STREAK IN HIM. . .

YEAH, I KNOW. I'M JUST BEGINNING TO FIND OUT JUST HOW DEEP IT GOES.

I wandered around like a lost soul for days, trying desperately to find some kind of answer.

IF IT'S NOT SOMETHING OUTSIDE OF ME AND ALEX, LIKE ANOTHER GIRL, THEN IT MUST BE SOME-THING TO DO WITH US. . .

It had to be some-thing Alex could see but I couldn't. . .

OF COURSE, IT'S ME! IT'S SOME WAY IN WHICH I'VE CHANGED, OR MAYBE IT WAS SOMETHING I DID OR SAID.

Then I remembered, we had had a sort of row, several weeks ago.

HEY, ALEX, HAVE YOU SEEN THIS PLACE? TINA TOLD ME THE FOOD'S GREAT AND THEY PLAY REALLY GOOD MUSIC. IT'S VERY ROMANTIC, SHE RECKONS.

YEAH, AND VERY PRICEY TOO. WE SPEND ENOUGH GOING OUT AS IT IS, EMMA. I CAN'T AFFORD PLACES LIKE THAT TOO.

COME ON, YOU OLD SKINFLINT. WE COULD ALWAYS GO THERE FOR MY BIRTHDAY.

EMMA, YOU DON'T UNDERSTAND, I'M NOT JOKING. I REALLY CAN'T RUN TO PLACES LIKE THAT.

YEAH, BUT YOU BOUGHT THAT COMPACT DISC PLAYER LAST MONTH, DIDN'T YOU?

OH COME OFF IT, THAT WAS A ONE OFF. I DON'T BUY MYSELF THINGS LIKE THAT VERY OFTEN. AND AS IT WAS IN THE SALE, I HAD TO BUY IT THEN AND THERE.

169

IT'S TOO MUCH FOR ANY RELATIONSHIP TO STAND. IT'S DRAGGING ON, BUT THEY WON'T ADMIT IT. THEY'LL END UP HATING EACH OTHER. IF THEY'D HAD A CLEAN BREAK IN THE FIRST PLACE, THEY'D JUST REMEMBER THE GOOD TIMES NOW.

I knew that Alex was being cruel to be kind. He wanted to save me all the things his sister had been through.

BUT I'VE GOT A SOLUTION TO THE WHOLE THING!

I ran like mad, and caught him just as he was leaving for work.

ALEX, WAIT, IT'S ME! I HAVE TO TALK TO YOU.

EMMA. . .?

I had to grab hold of him, just to reassure myself he wouldn't run away.

ALEX, WHY DIDN'T YOU TELL ME ABOUT SWINDON? I THOUGHT IT WAS ANOTHER GIRL OR SOMETHING SERIOUS. YOUR BOSS HAS TOLD ME EVERYTHING.

BUT IT **IS** SERIOUS. I'LL BE LIVING A TWO HOUR JOURNEY AWAY FROM HERE. WE'D NEVER SEE EACH OTHER. IT WOULD JUST DRAG ON UNTIL IT DIED. IT'S HOPELESS.

I used every argument I could think of.

YOU CAN'T JUDGE THINGS BY YOUR SISTER. SHE AND ROB WERE BORED WITH EACH OTHER BEFORE SHE WENT AWAY. THEY DIDN'T LOVE EACH OTHER LIKE WE DO.

BUT YOU HAVE NO IDEA OF THE DIFFICULTIES, THE TRAVELLING, THE EXPENSE AND IF YOU CAME FOR THE WEEKEND WHERE WOULD YOU STAY?

Then I hit him with the clincher.

I'VE GOT AN AUNT WHO LIVES IN SWINDON. I CAN STAY WITH HER WHENEVE I LIKE. SO YOU SEE, THICKC WE CAN MAKE IT WORK. IF WE WANT TO. I'VE GOT A STUDENT RAILCARD, TOO. THEY'LL BE NO EXPENSE.

YOU NEVER TOLD ME THIS BEFORE.

HOW COULD I? YOU NEVER GAVE ME A CHANCE!

I could see I'd persuaded him.

It was wonderful — the kiss I'd never expected to have.

Now that I knew Alex's secret, I was sure everything would work out fine.

I CAN'T HELP THINKING I WAS CRAZY TO BELIEVE I COULD DO WITHOUT YOU.

WELL, YOU CAME TO YOUR SENSES IN THE END, THAT'S THE MAIN THING.

Mind you I did have a little secret of my own.

SO WHAT IF I HAVEN'T GOT AN AUNT IN SWINDON OR A STUDENT RAILCARD? NOW THAT I KNOW HE LOVES ME, THERE'S NO WAY I'M LETTING HIM FINISH WITH ME. I'VE COME TOO FAR TO GIVE UP NOW.

I was going to prove Alex wrong, I was going t make it work. Okay, he'd be mad when he fou out I was fibbing but that was a small price to pay. I knew he loved me and I would find a way — whatever. . .

THE END

171

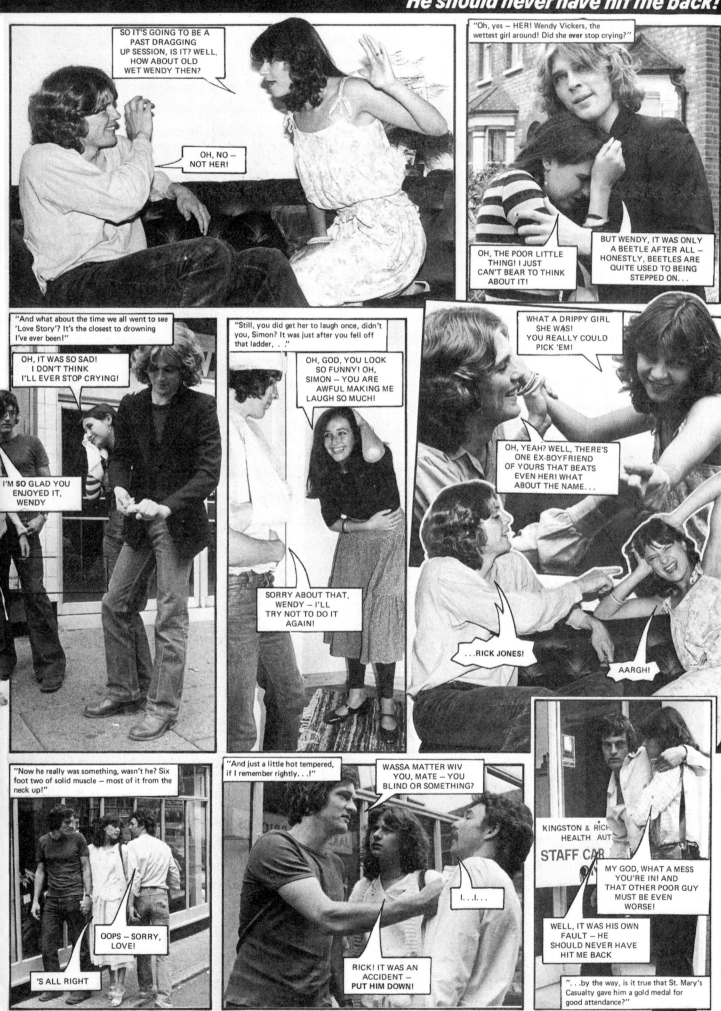

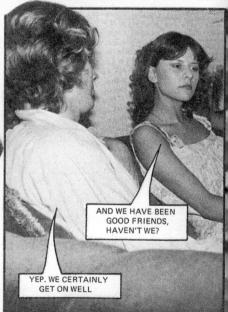

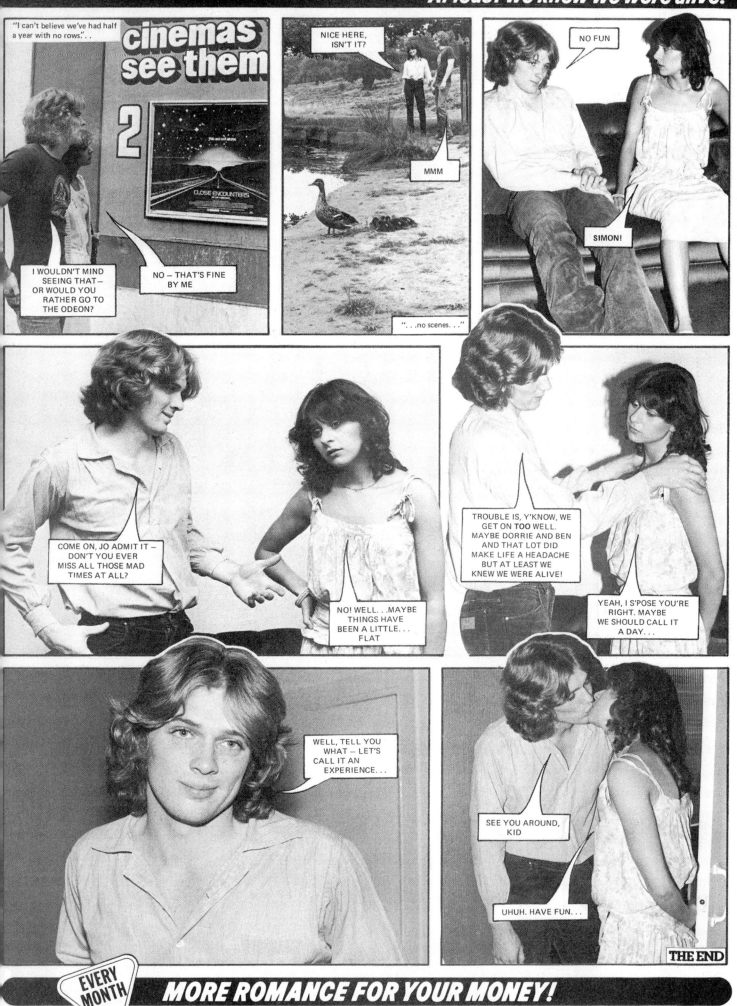

FAR FROM HOME

James and Sara would soon be going their separate ways...

James and Sara are two tourists from Oz who've met up in London. But on a day trip to Rye they discover they've got more in common than just travelling the world...

The moment passed.

ER, I THINK I'VE SEEN ENOUGH NOW.

YEAH, ME TOO.

OH WOW! WHAT A WHOLE BUNCH OF OLDE WORLDE ROOF TOPS.

He was about to kiss her, then...

HEY, HONEY! COME AND LOOK AT THIS. ARE THESE GREAT VIEWS OR WHAT!

177

AUTUMN BAY

The Story So Far: Boy mad Stefi Papageorgis split with boyfriend Neil just hours before a vital brain operation. Now, racked with guilt, she wants him back. But after snogging Stefi's half sister Bekkii, he's not so sure...

182

THE END

I'd been going out with Sean since November. I liked to think we were as close as any two people who'd been going out for almost a year.

...ut what was ...bout to happen ...ade me realise ...at I didn't ...now him as ...ell as I ...hought.

And that sharing pain and suffering can really bring you together.

And now when I listen to other people who say 'Oh, I'm really close to my boyfriend', I think, 'you don't know at all'. But I don't say anything.

Let them think that. Maybe one day they'll find out the way I did.

DYING YOUNG

The future was *too* painful to talk about....

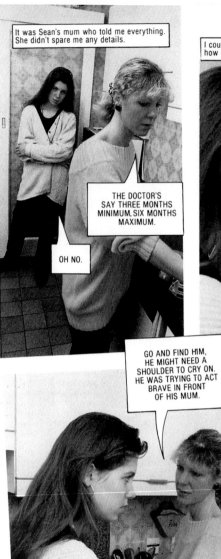

It was Sean's mum who told me everything. She didn't spare me any details.

THE DOCTOR'S SAY THREE MONTHS MINIMUM, SIX MONTHS MAXIMUM.

OH NO.

I couldn't believe how calm she was.

I'M SURE SEAN WOULD HAVE TOLD YOU, BUT IT'S BETTER COMING FROM ME. HE HASN'T TAKEN THE NEWS TOO WELL.

I suppose she'd known for much longer.

I felt numb.

W-WHERE IS HE NOW?

I DON'T KNOW, HE WENT OUT.

GO AND FIND HIM, HE MIGHT NEED A SHOULDER TO CRY ON. HE WAS TRYING TO ACT BRAVE IN FRONT OF HIS MUM.

I must have walked for an hour before I found him.

YOU'LL FREEZE YOU WILL.

I was expecting him to say something, even 'hello' but all he did was look at me, with eyes I hadn't seen before.

I couldn't say the words I wanted to. My voice sounded stupid.

YOU'RE MUM TOLD ME. . . ABOUT. . . WELL EVERYTHING.

I CAN'T BELIEVE IT.

NO, NEITHER CAN I.

184

ONE FROM THE HEART

SHE'S A COME-ON!

Dear Laura,
I fancy this girl at school. She's going out with someone, but she still shows interest in me, well sometimes! Then she just shuts down. Does she fancy me - or what?

I've known Kym Hughs for about two years.

For the last six months she's been going out with Matthew Smith.

I've fancied her since I knew her, but I've never done anything about it.

SHE'S LATE IF SHE'S GOING INTO FIFTH YEAR ASSEMBLY.

I haven't thought anything of it. Apart from 'I wish'.

Except smile.

HI.

OH, HI ALISTAIR.

IF ONLY.

Or at least I hadn't till last week.

And she smiles back, which she doesn't do with everybody.

YOU'RE GOING TO BE LATE.

OH WOW, WHAT A DRAAGI RUINED MY WHOLE DAY!

I couldn't believe what was happening.

YOU'VE GOT A REALLY LONG LIFE LINE. YOU'RE JUST GOING TO GO ON AND ON.

. . . AND ARISTON, YEAH. IS THIS THE LATEST HOBBY?

DOESN'T LOOK LIKE YOU'RE GOING TO BE VERY RICH, THOUGH.

HEY, THAT TICKLES.

IT CAN'T.

She'd never done anything like it before.

GIVE US YOUR HAND ALISTAIR, I'M READING PALMS.

GO ON THEN.

It had to be a come-on, it couldn't have been anything else.

KEEP STILL.

KYM - THERE YOU ARE. I'VE BEEN LOOKING ALL OVER SCHOOL.

188

Laura Downey Writes

I don't know. But I do know how you find out. Ask her out.

If she won't give you a straight answer, then forget it. She's more trouble than she's worth. The thing which really annoys flirts is, you not playing the game. This girl knows she can keep you hanging on. She shows you a bit of interest then you go lolloping after her like a big shaggy dog with your tongue hanging out.

It's probably just an ego boost for her. She's been going out with one boy for some time and she wants to test that she's still got pulling power. Only she knows if she wants out of the relationship she's in.

So call her bluff and ask her.

TOP

Star of *American Idol*, Cat Deeley g
fashion cameras, modelling all kinds

○ White T-shirt:
Fruit of the loom £6.99
Hooded sleeveless top:
Pepe £27.99
Pedal pushers: as main pic
Boots Converse
○ Red hooded top:
Champion £39.99
Red shorts with stripe:
Boyz 2 £13.99

○ Red and Black
baseball top:
Boyz 2 £17.99
Black shorts:
Boyz 2 £6.99
○ Baseball top:
Boyz 2 £17.99
Black tracksuit
bottoms:
Champion £19.99

Loom £13.99
White leggings
Fruit Of The Loom £10.99
(Tel: 0952 587123)

hrough patchwork
ippy Chick £25.99
Tel: 071-436 7128
aces: Janet Coles
Tel: 071-589 6667
ess: Hippy Chick
details as above
ohn Lewis £3.99

◗ Black top:
Essential Teens £13.99
Flares: Hippy Chick £28.99
Necklace: River Island £4.99
Red shoes: Shelly's £39.99
◗ Blue cropped top: Etam £8.99
Patchwork skirt: Etam £16.99
Green shoes: Shelly's £39.99
Flower: John Lewis £3.99
Waist jewellery: Janet Coles

191

Acknowledgements

The list of photostory contributors over a period of 19 years is enormous. Many people appeared in a number of issues of *My Guy*, in particular the photo-soaps; *Sisters*, *Clare*, *Away from Home*, *Saintbridge* and *Kingsbrook*.

Photographers: David Watts, Gary Compton, Mike Prior, Henry Arden, Karin Simons, Sven Arnstein, Dick Palmer.

Model finders: Hemma & Michael Sullivan, Wendy Milligan, Starnest.

Writers: Eve Lynn-Hill, Hamish Dawson, Sophie Tilly, Susan Welby, Fiona Soutar, Debbie Voller, John Monks, Simon Geller, John Harding.

Models: Vicki Aldred (*Truth Games*), Giles Aldred, Natalie Annettes, Natalie Baldwin, Chris Barrett, Frank Bastow, Rob Bastow, Emily Beevers, Simon Bennett, Kelly Beswick, Lucy Bing, Yolanda Binks, Quint Boa, Luke Boa, Louise Bowman, John Bridekirk (*Autumn Bay*), Tiffany Brown, Helena Chappell, Nichola Daden, Gina D'Angelo, Massimo D'Angelo, Jenny Darnell, Luke Doonan, Louisa Dowding, Sabrina Duncan, Helen Evans, Jamie Fearnley (*Autumn Bay*), James Fitchett (*Autumn Bay*), Lucy Foxell, Sally Geach, Emma Gell, Natalie Geller, Annabel Giles (*Murder By Numbers*), Sean Goldie, Ruth Gordon, Hugh Grant (*A Fool For His Love*), Piers Grundy, Lance Grundy, Ross Hadley, Simon Hall, Rebecca Harding, Paul Harrington, Sarah Harvey, Ashley Hayes, Liz Heery (*Borne on the Wind*), Emma Herbert, Verity Hogg, Chloe Hooper, Daniel Hopcroft, Theo Hopkinson (*Autumn Bay*), Isaac Hopkinson (*True Love Story*), Mureille Huard, Phil Humphrys, Tara Hutton, Craig Jameson, Scott Jameson (*Tales of the Riverbank*), Bhopindar Jaswal, Colin Jemmott, Alex Joannou, Selina Kidmond, Ideta Kimso, Dominic Knights, Emma Lampard, Kirsty Laremore (*Photographer's Assistant*), Vicky Lee-Bishop, Chris Leng, Susie Luckett, Tristan Mace, Leo Marriot, Carissa Maynard, Peter McKibben, Bill McMullen, Leonie Mellinger, Anna Milligan, Lorraine Milligan, James Milligan, Greg Moore (*If Leaving Me Is Easy*), Brian More (*Murder By Numbers*), Keith More, Chris Morton, Nadine Ogerman, 'Oggie', Dilly Orme, Lucy Owens, Susan Philby, Christina Pitts, Liana Pitts, Ben Pontin, Heidi Ponton, Alex Pursey (*When the Wind Blows*), Jo Pursey, Neil Reano, Saskia Reeves, Luke Richards, Marianne Rogers (*Autumn Bay*), Stefan Rzysko, Tomi Sackett (*Autumn Bay*), Joan Scarrot, Natalie Schavrien, Cindy Shelley, Rhona Small, Haydon Smith, Mark Smith (*The Way We Were*), Clare Smythe (*Toy Boy*), Hayley Stent, Christian Sullivan, 'Tayo', Lucy Taylor, Emma Taylor (*If Leaving Me is Easy*), Lucy Thumwood, Sarah Tough, Karen Turner, Sarah-Jane Varley, Samantha Webb, Carl Wermig, Hannah White (*Autumn Bay*), Claire Whittaker, Helena Whitehall, Maria Williams, Mark Williams, Vicky Wilkinson, Jessica Witchell, Christian Woodhouse, Emma Woolard, Charlotte Wootton, Sarah Wright, Toby Young.